POST-SYNODAL
APOSTOLIC EXHORTATION
ECCLESIA IN AMERICA
OF THE HOLY FATHER
JOHN PAUL II
TO THE BISHOPS,
PRIESTS AND DEACONS,
MEN AND WOMEN RELIGIOUS,
AND ALL THE LAY FAITHFUL
ON THE ENCOUNTER WITH THE LIVING JESUS CHRIST:
THE WAY TO CONVERSION,
COMMUNION AND SOLIDARITY
IN AMERICA

Publication No. 5-321
United States Catholic Conference
Washington, D.C.
ISBN 1-57455-321-6

Text and format from
LIBRERIA EDITRICE VATICANA
Vatican City

Published in the United States, February 1999

INDEX

INTRODUCTION [1] 3
How the Synod Assembly came about [2] . 5
The theme of the Assembly [3] 6
The celebration of the Assembly as an experience of
encounter [4] 7
Contributing to the unity of the continent [5] . 8
In the context of the new evangelization [6] . 9
With the presence and help of the Lord [7] . . 11

CHAPTER I

THE ENCOUNTER WITH
THE LIVING JESUS CHRIST

Encounters with the Lord in the New Testament [8] 13
Personal encounters and community encounters [9] 16
Encountering Christ in the time of the Church [10] 17
We encounter Jesus through Mary [11] . . . 19
Places of encounter with Christ [12] 21

CHAPTER II

ENCOUNTERING JESUS CHRIST
IN AMERICA TODAY

The situation of the men and women of America
and their encounter with the Lord [13] . . . 25
The Christian identity of America [14] 26
The fruits of holiness in America [15] . . . 27
Popular piety [16] 29
The Eastern Catholic presence [17] 31

The Church in the field of education and social
action [18] 32
Growing respect for human rights [19] . . 34
The phenomenon of globalization [20] . . . 35
Growing urbanization [21] 37
The burden of external debt [22] . . . 38
Corruption [23] 39
The drug trade [24] 40
Ecological concern [25] 41

CHAPTER III

THE PATH OF CONVERSION

The urgency of the call to conversion [26] . . 43
The social dimension of conversion [27] . . 45
Continuing conversion [28] 47
Guided by the Holy Spirit to a new way of living
[29] 48
The universal call to holiness [30] 51
Jesus, the one way to holiness [31] 52
Penance and reconciliation [32] 53

CHAPTER IV

THE PATH TO COMMUNION

The Church, sacrament of communion [33] . . 55
Christian initiation and communion [34] . . . 57
The Eucharist as center of communion with God
and with each other [35] 58
The Bishops as builders of communion [36] . . 60
Deeper communion between the particular Churches
[37] 61
Fraternal communion with the Eastern Catholic
Churches [38] 63
The priesthood as a sign of unity [39] . . . 64
Promoting vocations [40] 67
Renewing parishes [41] 69
Permanent deacons [42] 71
Consecrated life [43] 73
Lay faithful and the renewal of the Church [44] 74
The dignity of women [45] 78

Challenges facing Christian families [46] . . . 80
Young people, the hope of the future [47] . . 82
Leading children to encounter Christ [48] . 84
Elements of communion with other Christian
    Churches and Ecclesial Communities [49] . 85
The Church's relations with Jewish communities
    [50] 87
Non-Christian religions [51] 87

CHAPTER V
THE PATH TO SOLIDARITY

Solidarity, the fruit of communion [52] . . . 89
The Church's teaching, a statement of the demands
    of conversion [53] 90
The Church's social doctrine [54] 91
The globalization of solidarity [55] 93
Social sins which cry to heaven [56] . . 94
The ultimate foundation of human rights [57] 96
Preferential love for the poor and the outcast [58] 97
Foreign debt [59] 99
The fight against corruption [60] 100
The drug problem [61] 101
The arms race [62] 103
The culture of death and a society dominated by the
    powerful [63] 103
Discrimination against indigenous peoples and Amer-
    icans of African descent [64] 106
The question of immigrants [65] 108

CHAPTER VI
THE MISSION OF THE CHURCH
IN AMERICA TODAY:
THE NEW EVANGELIZATION

Sent by Christ [66] 110
Jesus Christ, the "good news" and the prime evan-
    gelizer [67] 112
The encounter with Christ spurs evangelization [68] 114
The importance of catechesis [69] 116
The evangelization of culture [70] 119

Evangelizing centers of education [71] . . . 120
Evangelization through the media [72] . . 123
The challenge of the sects [73] 125
The mission *ad gentes* [74] 128

CONCLUSION

With hope and gratitude [75] 131
Prayer to Jesus Christ for the families of America
[76] 132

INTRODUCTION

1.   R EJOICING IN THE FAITH received and praising Christ for this immense gift, the Church in America has recently celebrated the fifth centenary of the first preaching of the Gospel on its soil. The commemoration made all American Catholics more deeply aware of Christ's desire to meet the inhabitants of the so-called New World so that, gathering them into his Church, he might be present in the continent's history. The evangelization of America is not only a gift from the Lord; it is also a source of new responsibilities. Thanks to the work of those who preached the Gospel through the length and breadth of the continent, countless sons and daughters have been generated by the Church and the Holy Spirit.[1] Now, no less than in the past, the words of the Apostle echo in their hearts: "If I preach the Gospel, I have no reason

---

[1] In this regard, the ancient inscription in the Baptistery of Saint John Lateran is eloquent: "Virgineo foetu Genitrix Ecclesia natos / quos spirante Deo concipit amne parit" (E. DIEHL, *Inscriptiones Latinae Christianae Veteres*, No. 1513, I. I:, Berolini 1925, p. 289).

to boast. It is my duty: woe to me if I do not preach the Gospel!" (*1 Cor* 9:16). This duty is founded on the Risen Lord's command to the Apostles before he ascended into heaven: "Preach the Gospel to all creation" (*Mk* 16:15).

This command applies to the whole Church; and, in this moment of her history, the Church in America is called to take it up and respond with loving generosity to the fundamental task of evangelization. This was what my Predecessor Paul VI, the first Pope to visit America, stressed at Bogotà: "It will be our task, [Lord Jesus], as your representatives and stewards of your divine mysteries (cf. *1 Cor* 4:1; *1 Pt* 4:10), to spread among men the treasures of your word, your grace, your example".[2] For the disciple of Christ the duty to evangelize is an obligation of love. "The love of Christ impels us" (*2 Cor* 5:14), declares the Apostle Paul, recalling all that the Son of God did for us in his redeeming sacrifice: "One man has died for all . . . that those who live may live no longer for themselves, but for him who died and was raised for their sake" (*2 Cor* 5:14-15).

The celebration of anniversaries which evoke in a particular way Christ's love for us stirs in our soul not only a sense of gratitude but also a sense of the need to "proclaim the wonders of God", to evangelize. Thus, the recent celebration of the five hundredth anniversary of the coming

---

[2] Homily at the Ordination of Priests and Deacons at Bogotà (August 22, 1968): *AAS* 60 (1968), 614-615.

of the Gospel to America — the moment, that is, when Christ first called America to faith — and the approaching Jubilee, when the Church will celebrate the two thousandth anniversary of the Incarnation of the Son of God, are special times when our hearts spontaneously ring out in gratitude to the Lord. Realizing the greatness of the gifts received, the pilgrim Church in America wishes to bring the whole of society and every man and woman to share in the riches of faith and communion in Christ.

How the Synod Assembly came about

2.   On October 12, 1992, the very day marking the five hundredth anniversary of the first evangelization of America, I spoke at the opening of the Fourth General Assembly of the Latin American Bishops in Santo Domingo. With the aim of broadening perspectives and giving impetus to the new evangelization, I proposed a synodal meeting, "with a view to increased cooperation between the different particular Churches", so that together we might address, as part of the new evangelization and as an expression of episcopal communion, "the problems relating to justice and solidarity among all the nations of America".[3] The positive response to my suggestion from the Bishops' Conferences of America enabled me to propose in my Apostolic Letter *Ter-*

[3] No. 17: *AAS* 85 (1993), 820.

tio Millennio Adveniente a synodal meeting "on the problems of the new evangelization in both parts of the same continent, so different in origin and history, and on issues of justice and of international economic relations, in view of the enormous gap between North and South".[4] This paved the way for more immediate preparations, leading to the Special Assembly for America of the Synod of Bishops, which was held in the Vatican from November 16 to December 12, 1997.

The theme of the Assembly

3.   In keeping with the original idea, and after listening to the suggestions of the Pre-Synodal Council, which expressed the views of many Pastors of the People of God on the American continent, I announced the theme of the Special Assembly for America of the Synod in these words: *Encounter with the Living Jesus Christ: The Way to Conversion, Communion and Solidarity in America.* Put this way, the theme makes clear the centrality of the person of the Risen Christ, present in the life of the Church and calling people to conversion, communion and solidarity. The starting-point of such a program of evangelization is in fact the encounter with the Lord. Given by Christ in the Paschal Mystery, the Holy Spirit guides us towards those pastoral goals which the

[4] No. 38: *AAS* 87 (1995), 30.

Church in America must attain in the third Christian millennium.

The celebration of the Assembly
as an experience of encounter

4.   It is certain that the Assembly was an expe rience of encounter with the Lord. I have especially happy memories of the two Solemn Concelebrations at which I presided in Saint Peter's Basilica at the opening and closing of the Assembly proceedings. Contact with the Risen Lord, truly, really and substantially present in the Eucharist, generated the spiritual atmosphere which enabled the Bishops taking part in the Synodal Assembly to see themselves not only as brothers in the Lord but also as members of the College of Bishops, eager to follow in the footsteps of the Good Shepherd under the leadership of the Successor of Peter, and serving the Church as she makes her pilgrim way in every corner of the continent. None could fail to see the joy of the participants, as they found the Assembly an extraordinary moment of encounter with the Lord, with the Vicar of Christ, with so many Bishops, priests, religious and lay people from every part of the continent.

To be sure, a number of earlier events contributed in a preliminary but powerful way to creating an atmosphere of fraternal encounter in the Synodal Assembly. First, there were the prior experiences of communion in the General Assemblies of the Bishops of Latin America in Rio de Janeiro (1955), Medellin (1968), Puebla (1979) and Santo Domingo (1992). These were moments when the Pastors of the Church in Latin America were able to reflect together as brothers on the most urgent pastoral questions affecting that part of the continent. There are also the periodic pan-American meetings of Bishops, in which the participants can address issues affecting the entire continent, and exchange views on the common problems and challenges facing the Church in the countries of America.

Contributing to the unity of the continent

5.   In Santo Domingo, when I first proposed a Special Assembly of the Synod, I remarked that "on the threshold of the third Christian millennium and at a time when many walls and ideological barriers have fallen, the Church feels absolutely duty-bound to bring into still deeper spiritual union the peoples who compose this great continent and also, prompted by the religious mission which is proper to the Church, to stir among these peoples a spirit of solidarity".[5] I asked that the Special Assembly of the Synod of Bishops reflect on America as a single entity, by reason of all that is common to the peoples of the continent, including their shared Christian identity and

[5] Address at the Opening of the Fourth General Conference of Latin American Bishops (October 12, 1992), 17: *AAS* 85 (1993), 820-821.

their genuine attempt to strengthen the bonds of solidarity and communion between the different forms of the continent's rich cultural heritage. The decision to speak of "America" in the singular was an attempt to express not only the unity which in some way already exists, but also to point to that closer bond which the peoples of the continent seek and which the Church wishes to foster as part of her own mission, as she works to promote the communion of all in the Lord.

In the context of the new evangelization

6.   With an eye to the Great Jubilee of the Year 2000, I was keen that there should be a Special Assembly of the Synod of Bishops for each of the five continents: after the Assembly for Africa (1994), America (1997), Asia (1998) and most recently Oceania (1998), in 1999 there will be, with the Lord's help, a Special Assembly for Europe. This will make possible an Ordinary General Assembly during the Jubilee year, to identify the rich insights which have come from the continental Assemblies and synthesize the conclusions to be drawn from them. That will be possible because similar concerns and points of interest have emerged from all the Synods. In this regard, referring to this series of Synodal Assemblies, I noted how "the theme underlying them all is *evangelization*, or rather *the new evangelization*, the foundations of which were laid

down in the Apostolic Exhortation *Evangelii Nuntiandi* of Pope Paul VI".[6] And so, in both my initial proposal to hold this Special Assembly of the Synod, and later in announcing the Synod itself, and after the Bishops' Conferences of America had agreed to the idea, I suggested that the Assembly's deliberations should address "the area of the new evangelization",[7] and the problems emerging from it.[8]

This concern was all the more prominent, given that I myself had outlined an initial program for a new evangelization on American soil. As the Church throughout America prepared to commemorate the five hundredth anniversary of the first evangelization of the continent, when speaking to the Council of Latin American Bishops in Port-au-Prince (Haiti), I had said: "The commemoration of the five hundred years of evangelization will achieve its full meaning if it becomes a commitment by you the Bishops, together with your priests and people, a commitment not to a re-evangelization but to a new evangelization — new in ardor, methods and expression".[9] Later, I invited the whole Church to respond to this call, although the program of

[6] JOHN PAUL II, Apostolic Letter *Tertio Millennio Adveniente* (November 10, 1994), 21: *AAS* 87 (1995), 17.

[7] Address at the Opening of the Fourth General Conference of Latin American Bishops (October 12, 1992), 17: *AAS* 85 (1993), 820.

[8] Cf. Apostolic Letter *Tertio Millennio Adveniente* (November 10, 1994), 21: *AAS* 87 (1995), 17.

[9] Address to the Assembly of CELAM (March 9, 1983), III: *AAS* 75 (1983), 778.

evangelization, embracing today's world in all its diversity, must take different shape in the light of two quite different situations: on the one hand, the situation of countries strongly affected by secularization, and, on the other, the situation of countries where there are still "many vital traditions of piety and popular forms of Christian religiosity".[10] There is no doubt that in varying degrees both these situations are present in different countries or, better perhaps, in different groups within the various countries of the American continent.

With the presence and help of the Lord

7.   With the command to evangelize which the Risen Lord left to his Church there goes the certitude, founded on his promise, that he continues to live and work among us: "I am with you always, to the close of the age" (*Mt* 28:20). The mysterious presence of Christ in his Church is the sure guarantee that the Church will succeed in accomplishing the task entrusted to her. At the same time, this presence enables us to encounter him, as the Son sent by the Father, as the Lord of Life who gives us his Spirit. A fresh encounter with Jesus Christ will make all the members of the Church in America aware that they are called to continue the Redeemer's mission in their lands.

[10] Post-Synodal Apostolic Exhortation *Christifideles Laici* (December 30, 1988), 34: *AAS* 81 (1989), 454.

If it is genuine, the personal encounter with the Lord will also bring a renewal of the Church: as sisters and neighbors to each other, the particular Churches of the continent will strengthen the bonds of cooperation and solidarity in order that the saving work of Christ may continue in the history of America with ever greater effect. Open to the unity which comes from true communion with the Risen Lord, the particular Churches, and all who belong to them, will discover through their own spiritual experience that "the encounter with the living Jesus Christ" is "the path to conversion, communion and solidarity". To the extent that these goals are reached, there will emerge an ever increasing dedication to the new evangelization of America.

CHAPTER I

THE ENCOUNTER WITH
THE LIVING JESUS CHRIST

"We have found the Messiah" (*Jn* 1:41)

Encounters with the Lord in the New Testament

8.   The Gospels relate many meetings between
Jesus and the men and women of his day. A
common feature of all these narratives is the
transforming power present and manifest in these
encounters with Jesus, inasmuch as they "initiate
an authentic process of conversion, communion
and solidarity" [11] Among the most significant is
the meeting with the Samaritan woman (cf.
Jn 4:5-42). Jesus calls her in order to quench his
thirst, a thirst which was not only physical: indeed, "he who asked for a drink was thirsting
for the faith of that woman".[12] By saying to her
"Give me a drink" (*Jn* 4:7) and speaking to her
about living water, the Lord awakened in the
Samaritan woman a question, almost a prayer for
something far greater than she was capable of
understanding at the time: "Sir, give me this wa-

[11] *Propositio 3*.
[12] Saint Augustine, *Tract. In Ioh.* 15, 11: *CCL* 36, 154.

13

ter, that I may not thirst" (*Jn* 4:15). The Samaritan woman, even though "she does not yet understand",[13] is in fact asking for the living water of which her divine visitor speaks. When Jesus reveals to her that he is indeed the Christ (cf. *Jn* 4:26), the Samaritan woman feels impelled to proclaim to the other townspeople that she has found the Messiah (cf. *Jn* 4:28-30). Similarly, the most precious fruit of the encounter between Jesus and Zacchaeus (cf. *Lk* 19:1-10) is the conversion of the tax collector, who becomes aware of his past unjust actions and decides to make abundant restitution — "four times as much" — to those he had cheated. Furthermore, he adopts an attitude of detachment from material goods and of charity towards the needy, which leads him to give half of his possessions to the poor.

Special mention should be made of the encounters with the Risen Jesus reported in the New Testament. Mary Magdalen meets the Risen One, and as a result overcomes her discouragement and grief at the death of the Master (cf. *Jn* 20:11-18). In his new Paschal glory, Jesus tells her to proclaim to the disciples that he has risen: "Go to my brethren" (*Jn* 20:17). For this reason, Mary Magdalen could be called "the apostle of the Apostles".[14] The disciples of Emmaus, for

[13] *Ibid.*, 15, 17: *loc. cit.*, 156.

[14] "Salvator ... ascensionis suae eam (Mariam Magdalenam) ad apostolos instituit apostolam". RABANUS MAURUS, *De Vita Beatae Mariae Magdalenae*, 27: PL 112, 1574. Cf. SAINT PETER DAMIAN, *Sermo 56*: PL 144, 820; HUGH OF CLUNY, *Commoni-*

their part, after meeting and recognizing the Risen Lord, return to Jerusalem to recount to the Apostles and the other disciples all that had happened to them (cf. *Lk* 24:13-35). Jesus, "beginning with Moses and all the prophets, interpreted to them in all the scriptures the things concerning himself" (*Lk* 24:27). Later they would recognize that their hearts were burning within them as the Lord talked to them along the road and opened the Scriptures to them (cf. *Lk* 24:32). There is no doubt that Saint Luke, in relating this episode, especially the decisive moment in which the two disciples recognize Jesus, makes explicit allusion to the accounts of the institution of the Eucharist by Jesus at the Last Supper (cf. *Lk* 24:30). The Evangelist, in relating what the disciples of Emmaus told the Eleven, uses an expression which had a precise Eucharistic meaning for the early Church: "He was made known to them in the breaking of the bread" (*Lk* 24:35).

One of the encounters with the Risen Lord which had a decisive influence on the history of Christianity was certainly the conversion of Saul, the future Paul, the Apostle of the Gentiles, on the road to Damascus. There his life was radically changed: from being a persecutor, he became an Apostle (cf. *Acts* 9:3-30; 22:6-11; 26:12-18). Paul himself describes this extraordinary experience as a revelation of the Son of God "in order

torium: PL 159, 952; SAINT THOMAS AQUINAS, *In Ioh. Evang. Expositio*, c. 20, l. 3.

15

that I might preach him among the Gentiles" (*Gal* 1:16).

The Lord always respects the freedom of those he calls. There are cases where people, in encountering Jesus, close their hearts to the change of life to which the Lord is calling them. Many people in Jesus's own time saw and heard him, and yet did not open their hearts to his word. Saint John's Gospel points to sin as the reason which prevents human beings from opening themselves to the light which is Christ: "the light has come into the world, and people loved darkness rather than light, because their deeds were evil" (*Jn* 3:19). The Gospels teach that attachment to wealth is an obstacle to accepting Christ's call to follow him fully and without reserve. Here, the attitude of the rich young man is indicative (cf. *Mt* 19:16-22; *Mk* 10:17-22; *Lk* 18:18-23).

Personal encounters and community encounters

9.   Some of the encounters with Jesus mentioned in the Gospel are clearly personal, as, for example, when he summons someone to follow him (cf. *Mt* 9:9; *Mk* 2:13-14; *Lk* 5:27-28). In these cases, Jesus deals familiarly with his hearers: "'Rabbi (which means teacher), where are you staying?' . . . 'Come and see'" (*Jn* 1:38-39). But at other times the encounters are communal in nature. This is especially true of the encounters with the Apostles, which are of fundamental

importance for the constitution of the Church. Indeed, the Apostles, chosen by Jesus from among the wider circle of his disciples (cf. *Mk* 3:13-19; *Lk* 6:12-16), receive special training and enjoy a closer relationship with him. To the crowds Jesus speaks in parables, while explaining to the Twelve: "To you it has been given to know the secrets of the kingdom of heaven, but to them it has not been given" (*Mt* 13:11). They are called to be heralds of the Good News and to carry out a special mission of building up the Church by the grace of the sacraments. To this end, they receive the necessary power: Jesus confers upon them the authority to forgive sins, invoking the same authority which the Father has given him in heaven and on earth (cf. *Mt* 28:18). They would be the first to receive the gift of the Holy Spirit (cf. *Acts* 2:1-4), a gift then bestowed upon all who by virtue of the Sacraments of Initiation would become part of the Christian community (cf. *Acts* 2:38).

Encountering Christ in the time of the Church

10.   The Church is the place where men and women, by encountering Jesus, can come to know the love of the Father, for whoever has seen Jesus has seen the Father (cf. *Jn* 14:9). After his Ascension into heaven, Jesus acts through the powerful agency of the Holy Spirit, the Paraclete (cf. *Jn* 16:17), who transforms believers by giving them new life. Thus they become capable

of loving with God's own love, which "has been poured into our hearts through the Holy Spirit which has been given to us" (*Rom* 5:5). God's grace also enables Christians to work for the transformation of the world, in order to bring about a new civilization, which my Predecessor Paul VI appropriately called "the civilization of love".[15]

Indeed, "the Word of God, by taking on our human nature in all things save sin (cf. *Heb* 4:15), manifests the Father's plan by revealing to each human person the way to realize fully his or her vocation. Thus Jesus not only reconciles man with the Father, but also reconciles man with himself and thus reveals his true nature".[16] With these words the Synod Fathers, taking up the teaching of the Second Vatican Council, reaffirmed that Jesus is the way which leads to full personal realization, culminating in the definitive and eternal encounter with God. "I am the way, and the truth, and the life; no one comes to the Father, but by me" (*Jn* 14:6). God has predestined us "to be conformed to the image of his Son, in order that he might be the first-born of many brethren" (*Rom* 8:29). Jesus Christ is thus the definitive answer to the question of the meaning of life, and to those fundamental ques-

[15] Address for the Closing of the Holy Year (December 25, 1975): *AAS* 68 (1976), 145.

[16] *Propositio* 9; cf. SECOND VATICAN ECUMENICAL COUNCIL, Pastoral Constitution on the Church in the Modern World *Gaudium et Spes*, 22.

tions which still trouble so many men and women on the American continent.

We encounter Jesus through Mary

11.   At the birth of Jesus, the Magi came from the East to Bethlehem and "saw the child with Mary his Mother" (*Mt* 2:11). At the beginning of his public life, at the marriage of Cana, when the Son of God works the first of his signs, awakening faith in the disciples (cf. *Jn* 2:11), it is Mary who intervenes and directs the servants towards her Son in these words: "Do whatever he tells you" (*Jn* 2:5). In this regard I once wrote that "the Mother of Christ presents herself as the *spokeswoman of her Son's will*, pointing out those things which must be done so that the salvific power of the Messiah may be manifested".[17] For this reason Mary is the sure path to our meeting with Christ. Devotion to the Mother of the Lord, when it is genuine, is always an impetus to a life guided by the spirit and values of the Gospel.

How can we fail to emphasize the role which belongs to the Virgin Mary in relation to the pilgrim Church in America journeying towards its encounter with the Lord? Indeed, the Most Blessed Virgin "is linked in a special way to the birth of the Church in the history ... of the

[17] Encyclical Letter *Redemptoris Mater* (March 25, 1987), 21: *AAS* 79 (1987), 369.

peoples of America; through Mary they came to encounter the Lord".[18]

Throughout the continent, from the time of the first evangelization, the presence of the Mother of God has been strongly felt, thanks to the efforts of the missionaries. In their preaching, "the Gospel was proclaimed by presenting the Virgin Mary as its highest realization. From the beginning — invoked as Our Lady of Guadalupe — Mary, by her motherly and merciful figure, was a great sign of the closeness of the Father and of Jesus Christ, with whom she invites us to enter into communion".[19]

The appearance of Mary to the native Juan Diego on the hill of Tepeyac in 1531 had a decisive effect on evangelization.[20] Its influence greatly overflows the boundaries of Mexico, spreading to the whole Continent. America, which historically has been, and still is, a melting-pot of peoples, has recognized in the *mestiza* face of the Virgin of Tepeyac, "in Blessed Mary of Guadalupe, an impressive example of a perfectly inculturated evangelization".[21] Consequently, not only in Central and South America, but in North America as

[18] *Propositio* 5.

[19] THIRD GENERAL CONFERENCE OF THE LATIN AMERICAN BISHOPS, Puebla, February 1979, *Message to the Peoples of Latin America*, No. 282. For the United States, cf. NATIONAL CONFERENCE OF CATHOLIC BISHOPS, Pastoral Letter *Behold Your Mother. Woman of Faith* (Washington, 1973), p. 37.

[20] *Propositio* 6.

[21] JOHN PAUL II, Address at the Opening of the Fourth General Conference of Latin American Bishops (October 12, 1992), 24: *AAS* 85 (1993), 826.

well, the Virgin of Guadalupe is venerated as Queen of all America.[22]

With the passage of time, pastors and faithful alike have grown increasingly conscious of the role of the Virgin Mary in the evangelization of America. In the prayer composed for the Special Assembly for America of the Synod of Bishops, Holy Mary of Guadalupe is invoked as "Patroness of all America and Star of the first and new evangelization". In view of this, I welcome with joy the proposal of the Synod Fathers that the feast of Our Lady of Guadalupe, Mother and Evangelizer of America, be celebrated throughout the continent on December 12.[23] It is my heartfelt hope that she, whose intercession was responsible for strengthening the faith of the first disciples (cf. *Jn* 2:11), will by her maternal intercession guide the Church in America, obtaining the outpouring of the Holy Spirit, as she once did for the early Church (cf. *Acts* 1:14), so that the new evangelization may yield a splendid flowering of Christian life.

Places of encounter with Christ

12. Trusting in the help of Mary, the Church in America desires to lead the men and women of the continent to encounter Christ. This encounter will be the starting-point of authentic

---

[22] Cf. NATIONAL CONFERENCE OF CATHOLIC BISHOPS, *Behold Your Mother. Woman of Faith* (Washington, 1973), 37.

[23] Cf. *Propositio* 6.

conversion and of renewed communion and solidarity. Such an encounter will contribute greatly to strengthening the faith of many Catholics, helping them to mature in strong, lively and active faith.

Lest the search for Christ present in his Church become something merely abstract, we need to indicate the specific times and places in which, in the Church, it is possible to encounter him. Here the reflections of the Synod Fathers offered abundant suggestions and observations.

They pointed above all to "Sacred Scripture read in the light of Tradition, the Fathers and the Magisterium, and more deeply understood through meditation and prayer".[24] A recommendation was made to promote knowledge of the Gospels, which proclaim in words easily understood by all the way Jesus lived among the people of his time. Reading these sacred texts and listening to Jesus as attentively as did the multitudes of the mount of the Beatitudes, or on the shore of the Lake of Tiberias as he preached from the boat, produces authentic fruits of conversion of heart.

A second place of encounter with Jesus is the sacred Liturgy.[25] Thanks to the Second Vatican Council, we have a very rich account of the manifold presence of Christ in the Liturgy, the importance of which should lead to it being a theme of constant preaching. Christ is present in

[24] *Propositio* 4.
[25] Cf. *ibid.*

the celebrant who renews at the altar the one and only Sacrifice of the Cross; he is present in the Sacraments through which he exercises his efficacious power. When his word is proclaimed, it is he himself who speaks to us. He is also present in the community, by virtue of his promise that "where two or three are gathered in my name, there am I in the midst of them" (*Mt* 18:20). He is present "especially under the Eucharistic species".[26] My Predecessor Paul VI deemed it necessary to explain the uniqueness of Christ's real presence in the Eucharist, which "is called 'real' not to exclude the idea that the others are 'real' too, but rather to indicate presence *par excellence*, because it is substantial".[27] Under the species of bread and wine, "Christ is present, whole and entire in his physical 'reality', corporally present".[28]

The Scriptures and the Eucharist, places of encounter with Christ, are evoked in the story of the apparition of the Risen Jesus to the disciples of Emmaus. The Gospel text concerning the final judgment (cf. *Mt* 25:31-46), which states that we will be judged on our love towards the needy in whom the Lord Jesus is mysteriously present, indicates that we must not neglect a third place of encounter with Christ: "the persons, especially

[26] Cf. SECOND VATICAN ECUMENICAL COUNCIL, Dogmatic Constitution on the Sacred Liturgy *Sacrosanctum Concilium*, 7.

[27] Encyclical Letter *Mysterium Fidei* (September 3, 1965): *AAS* 57 (1965), 764.

[28] *Ibid.*, *loc. cit.*, 766.

the poor, with whom Christ identifies himself".[29] At the closing of the Second Vatican Council, Pope Paul VI recalled that "on the face of every human being, especially when marked by tears and sufferings, we can and must see the face of Christ (cf. *Mt* 25:40), the Son of Man".[30]

[29] *Propositio* 4.
[30] Address at the Final Public Session of the Second Vatican Council (December 7, 1965): *AAS* 58 (1966), 58.

CHAPTER II

ENCOUNTERING JESUS CHRIST IN AMERICA TODAY

"From those who have received much, much will be required" (*Lk* 12:48)

The situation of the men and women of America and their encounter with the Lord

13.   The Gospels tell of Jesus encountering people in very diverse situations. At times these are situations of sin, which show the need for conversion and the Lord's forgiveness. At other moments we find people searching for the truth and genuinely trusting in Jesus — positive attitudes which help to establish a friendship with him and awaken the desire to imitate him. Nor can we forget the gifts with which the Lord prepares some people for a later encounter. Thus, by making Mary "full of grace" (*Lk* 1:28) from the very beginning, God prepared her for the realization in her of God's supreme encounter with human nature: the ineffable mystery of the Incarnation.

Like the social virtues, sins do not exist in the abstract, but are the consequence of personal acts.[31] Hence it is necessary to bear in mind that America today is a complex reality, the result of the attitudes and actions of the men and women who live there. It is in this real and concrete situation that they must encounter Jesus.

The Christian identity of America

14.   The greatest gift which America has received from the Lord is the faith which has forged its Christian identity. For more than five hundred years the name of Christ has been proclaimed on the continent. The evangelization which accompanied the European migrations has shaped America's religious profile, marked by moral values which, though they are not always consistently practiced and at times are cast into doubt, are in a sense the heritage of all Americans, even of those who do not explicitly recognize this fact. Clearly, America's Christian identity is not synonymous with Catholic identity. The presence of other Christian communities, to a greater or lesser degree in the different parts of America, means that the ecumenical commitment to seek unity among

[31] Cf. JOHN PAUL II, Apostolic Exhortation *Reconciliatio et Paenitentia* (December 2, 1984), 16: *AAS* 77 (1985), 214-217.

all those who believe in Christ is especially urgent.[32]

The fruits of holiness in America

15. The Saints are the true expression and the finest fruits of America's Christian identity. In them, the encounter with the living Christ "is so deep and demanding . . . that it becomes a fire which consumes them completely and impels them to build his Kingdom, to the point that Christ and the new Covenant are the meaning and the soul . . . of personal and communal life".[33] The fruits of holiness have flourished from the first days of the evangelization of America. Thus we have Saint Rose of Lima (1586-1617), "the New World's first flower of holiness", proclaimed principal patroness of America in 1670 by Pope Clement X.[34] After her, the list of American saints has grown to its present length.[35]

[32] Cf. *Propositio* 61.

[33] *Propositio* 29.

[34] Cf. Bull *Sacrosancti Apostolatus Cura* (August 11, 1670), § 3: *Bullarium Romanum*, 26/VII, 42.

[35] Among others, we may mention the following: the martyrs John de Brébeuf and his seven companions, Roque Gonzales and his two companions; the saints Elizabeth Ann Seton, Marguerite Bourgeoys, Peter Claver, Juan de Castillo, Rose Philippine Duchesne, Marguerite d'Youville, Francisco Febres Cordero, Teresa Fernández Solar de las Andes, Juan Macías, Turibius of Mongrovejo, Ezechiel Moreno y Diaz, John Neumann, Maria Ana de Jesús Paredes y Flores, Martin de Porres, Alfonso Rodriguez, Francisco Solano, Frances Xavier Cabrini; and those beatified: José de Anchieta, Pedro de San José de Betancur, Juan Diego, Katharine Drexel, Maria de la Encarnación Rosal, Rafael Guizar Valencia, Dina Bélanger, Alberto Hurtado Cruchaga, Elias del Socorro Nieves, Maria Francisca de Jesús Rubatto, Mercede de Jesús Molina, Narcisa de Jesús Martillo Morán, Miguel Pro,

The beatifications and canonizations which have raised many sons and daughters of the continent to public veneration provide heroic models of the Christian life across the range of nations and social backgrounds. In beatifying or canonizing them, the Church points to them as powerful intercessors made one with Christ, the eternal High Priest, the mediator between God and man. The Saints and the Beatified of America accompany the men and women of today with fraternal concern in all their joys and sufferings, until the final encounter with the Lord.[36] With a view to encouraging the faithful to imitate them ever more closely and to seek their intercession more frequently and fruitfully, the Synod Fathers proposed — and I find this a very timely initiative — that there be prepared "a collection of short biographies of the Saints and the Beatified of America, which can shed light on and stimulate the response to the universal call to holiness in America".[37]

Among the Saints it has produced, "the history of the evangelization of America numbers many martyrs, men and women, Bishops and priests, consecrated religious and lay people who have given life . . . to [these] nations with their

Maria de San José Alvarado Cardozo, Junípero Serra, Kateri Tekakwitha, Laura Vicuña, Antônio de Sant'Anna Galvão and many others who have been beatified and whom the peoples of America invoke with faith and devotion (cf. Instrumentum Laboris, 17).

[36] Cf. SECOND ECUMENICAL VATICAN COUNCIL, Dogmatic Constitution on the Church Lumen Gentium, 50.

[37] Propositio 31.

blood. Like a cloud of witnesses (cf. *Heb* 12:1), they stir us to take up fearlessly and fervently today's task of the new evangelization".[38] Their example of boundless dedication to the cause of the Gospel must not only be saved from oblivion, but must become better and more widely known among the faithful of the continent. In this regard, I wrote in *Tertio Millennio Adveniente*: "The local Churches should do everything possible to ensure that the memory of those who have suffered martyrdom should be safeguarded, gathering the necessary documentation".[39]

Popular piety

16.   A distinctive feature of America is an intense popular piety, deeply rooted in the various nations. It is found at all levels and in all sectors of society, and it has special importance as a place of encounter with Christ for all those who in poverty of spirit and humility of heart are sincerely searching for God (cf. *Mt* 11:25). This piety takes many forms: "Pilgrimages to shrines of Christ, of the Blessed Virgin and the Saints, prayer for the souls in purgatory, the use of sacramentals (water, oil, candles . . .). These and other forms of popular piety are an opportunity for the faithful to encounter the living Christ".[40]

[38] *Propositio* 30.
[39] No. 37: *AAS* 87 (1995), 29; cf. *Propositio* 31.
[40] *Propositio* 21.

The Synod Fathers stressed the urgency of discovering the true spiritual values present in popular religiosity, so that, enriched by genuine Catholic doctrine, it might lead to a sincere conversion and a practical exercise of charity.[41] If properly guided, popular piety also leads the faithful to a deeper sense of their membership of the Church, increasing the fervor of their attachment and thus offering an effective response to the challenges of today's secularization.[42]

Given that in America, popular piety is a mode of inculturation of the Catholic faith and that it has often assumed indigenous religious forms, we must not underestimate the fact that, prudently considered, it too can provide valid cues for a more complete inculturation of the Gospel.[43] This is especially important among the indigenous peoples, in order that "the seeds of the Word" found in their culture may come to their fullness in Christ.[44] The same is true for Americans of African origin. The Church "recognizes that it must approach these Americans from within their own culture, taking seriously the spiritual and human riches of that culture which appear in the way they worship, their sense of

[41] Cf. *ibid*.
[42] Cf. *ibid*.
[43] Cf. *ibid*.
[44] Cf. *Propositio* 18.

joy and solidarity, their language and their traditions".[45]

The Eastern Catholic presence

17.   Immigration is an almost constant feature of America's history from the beginning of evangelization to our own day. As part of this complex phenomenon, we see that in recent times different parts of America have welcomed many members of the Eastern Catholic Churches who, for various reasons, have left their native lands. A first wave of immigration came especially from Western Ukraine; and then it involved the nations of the Middle East. This made it pastorally necessary to establish an Eastern Catholic hierarchy for these Catholic immigrants and their descendants. The Synod Fathers recalled the norms given by the Second Vatican Council, which recognize that the Eastern Churches "have the right and the duty to govern themselves according to their own particular discipline", given the mission they have of bearing witness to an ancient doctrinal, liturgical and monastic tradition. Moreover, these Churches have a duty to maintain their own disciplines, since these "correspond better to the customs of their faithful and are judged to be better suited to provide for the good of souls".[46]

---

[45] *Propositio* 19.

[46] Decree on the Eastern Catholic Churches *Orientalium Ecclesiarum*, 5; cf. *Code of Canons of the Eastern Churches*, Canon 28; *Propositio* 60.

31

The universal Church needs a *synergy* between the particular Churches of East and West so that she may breathe with her two lungs, in the hope of one day doing so in perfect communion between the Catholic Church and the separated Eastern Churches.[47] Therefore, we cannot but rejoice that the Eastern Churches have in recent times taken root in America alongside the Latin Churches present there from the beginning, thus making the catholicity of the Lord's Church appear more clearly.[48]

The Church in the field
of education and social action

18.   One of the reasons for the Church's influence on the Christian formation of Americans is her vast presence in the field of education and especially in the university world. The many Catholic universities spread throughout the continent are a typical feature of Church life in America. Also in the field of primary and secondary education, the large number of Catholic schools makes possible a wide-ranging evangelizing effort, as long as there is a clear will to impart a truly Christian education.[49]

[47] Cf. JOHN PAUL II, Apostolic Letter *Redemptoris Mater* (March 25, 1987), 34: *AAS* 79 (1987), 406; SYNOD OF BISHOPS, Special Assembly for Europe, Declaration *Ut Testes Simus Christi Qui Nos Liberavit* (December 13, 1991), III, 7: *Enchiridion Vaticanum* 13, 647-652.
[48] Cf. *Propositio* 60.
[49] Cf. *Propositiones* 23 and 24.

Another important area in which the Church is present in every part of America is social and charitable work. The many initiatives on behalf of the elderly, the sick and the needy, through nursing homes, hospitals, dispensaries, canteens providing free meals, and other social centers are a concrete testimony of the preferential love for the poor which the Church in America nurtures. She does so because of her love for the Lord and because she is aware that "Jesus identified himself with the poor (cf. *Mt* 25:31-46)".[50] In this task which has no limits, the Church in America has been able to create a sense of practical solidarity among the various communities of the continent and of the world, showing in this way the fraternal spirit which must characterize Christians in every time and place.

For this service of the poor to be both evangelical and evangelizing, it must faithfully reflect the attitude of Jesus, who came "to proclaim Good News to the poor" (*Lk* 4:18). When offered in this spirit, the service of the poor shows forth God's infinite love for all people and becomes an effective way of communicating the hope of salvation which Christ has brought to the world, a hope which glows in a special way when it is shared with those abandoned or rejected by society.

This constant dedication to the poor and disadvantaged emerges in the Church's social teach-

[50] *Propositio* 73.

ing, which ceaselessly invites the Christian community to a commitment to overcome every form of exploitation and oppression. It is a question not only of alleviating the most serious and urgent needs through individual actions here and there, but of uncovering the roots of evil and proposing initiatives to make social, political and economic structures more just and fraternal.

Growing respect for human rights

19.   Among the positive aspects of America today, we see in civil society a growing support throughout the continent for democratic political systems and the gradual retreat of dictatorial regimes; this has immediate moral implications. The Church looks sympathetically upon this evolution insofar as it favors an ever more marked respect for the rights of each individual, including those accused and condemned, against whom it is never legitimate to resort to modes of detention and investigation — one thinks especially of torture — which are offensive to human dignity. "The rule of law is the necessary condition for establishing true democracy".[51]

There can be no rule of law, however, unless citizens and especially leaders are convinced that there is no freedom without truth.[52] In effect,

[51] *Propositio* 72; cf. JOHN PAUL II, Encyclical Letter *Centesimus Annus* (May 1, 1991), 46: *AAS* 83 (1991), 850.
[52] Cf. SYNOD OF BISHOPS Special Assembly for Europe, Declaration *Ut Testes Simus Christi Qui Nos Liberavit* (December

"the grave problems which threaten the dignity of the human person, the family, marriage, education, the economy and working conditions, the quality of life and life itself, raise the question of the rule of law".[53] The Synod Fathers rightly stressed that "the fundamental rights of the human person are inscribed in human nature itself, they are willed by God and therefore call for universal observance and acceptance. No human authority can infringe upon them by appealing to majority opinion or political consensus, on the pretext of respect for pluralism and democracy. Therefore, the Church must be committed to the task of educating and supporting lay people in volved in law-making, government and the administration of justice, so that legislation will always reflect those principles and moral values which are in conformity with a sound anthropology and advance the common good".[54]

The phenomenon of globalization

20.   A feature of the contemporary world is the tendency towards globalization, a phenomenon which, although not exclusively American, is more obvious and has greater repercussions in America. It is a process made inevitable by increasing communication between the differ-

13, 1991), I, 1; II, 4; IV, 10; *Enchiridion Vaticanum* 13, 613-615; 627-633; 660-669.
   [53] *Propositio* 72.
   [54] *Ibid.*

ent parts of the world, leading in practice to overcoming distances, with evident effects in widely different fields.

The ethical implications can be positive or negative. There is an economic globalization which brings some positive consequences, such as efficiency and increased production and which, with the development of economic links between the different countries, can help to bring greater unity among peoples and make possible a better service to the human family. However, if globalization is ruled merely by the laws of the market applied to suit the powerful, the consequences cannot but be negative. These are, for example, the absolutizing of the economy, unemployment, the reduction and deterioration of public services, the destruction of the environment and natural resources, the growing distance between rich and poor, unfair competition which puts the poor nations in a situation of ever increasing inferiority.[55] While acknowledging the positive values which come with globalization, the Church considers with concern the negative aspects which follow in its wake.

And what should we say about the cultural globalization produced by the power of the media? Everywhere the media impose new scales of values which are often arbitrary and basically materialistic, in the face of which it is difficult to maintain a lively commitment to the values of the Gospel.

[55] Cf. *Propositio* 74.

21.   Also on the increase in America is the
phenomenon of urbanization. For some time now
the continent has been experiencing a constant
exodus from the countryside to the city. This is
a complex phenomenon already described by my
Predecessor Paul VI.[56] There are different reasons
for it, but chief among them are poverty and un-
derdevelopment in rural areas, where utilities,
transportation, and educational and health services are often inadequate. Moreover, the city,
with the allure of entertainment and prosperity
often presented in the media, exerts a special at-
traction for simple people from country areas.

The frequent lack of planning in this process
is a source of many evils. As the Synod Fathers
pointed out, "in certain cases, some urban areas
are like islands where violence, juvenile delin-
quency and an air of desperation flourish".[57] The
phenomenon of urbanization therefore presents
great challenges for the Church's pastoral action,
which must address cultural rootlessness, the loss
of family traditions and of people's particular religious traditions. As a result, faith is often weak-
ened because it is deprived of the expressions
that helped to keep it alive.

The evangelization of urban culture is a
formidable challenge for the Church. Just as she

[56] Cf. Apostolic Epistle *Octogesima Adveniens* (May 14,
1971), 8-9: *AAS* 63 (1971), 406-408.
[57] *Propositio* 35.

was able to evangelize rural culture for centuries, the Church is called in the same way today to undertake a methodical and far-reaching urban evangelization through catechesis, the liturgy and the very way in which her pastoral structures are organized.[58]

The burden of external debt

22.   The Synod Fathers voiced concern about the external debt afflicting many American nations and expressed solidarity with them. They were consistent in reminding public opinion of the complexity of this issue, acknowledging that "the debt is often the result of corruption and poor administration".[59] In keeping with the spirit of the Synod's deliberations, such an acknowledgment does not mean to place on one side all the blame for a phenomenon which is extremely complex in its origin and in the solutions which it demands.[60]

Among the causes which have helped to create massive external debt are not only high interest rates, caused by speculative financial policies, but also the irresponsibility of people in government who, in incurring debt, have given too little thought to the real possibility of repaying it. This

[58] Cf. *ibid.*

[59] *Propositio* 75.

[60] Cf. PONTIFICAL COMMISSION "IUSTITIA ET PAX", *At the Service of the Human Community: An Ethical Approach to the International Debt Question* (December 27, 1986): *Enchiridion Vaticanum* 10, 1045-1128.

has been aggravated by the fact that huge sums obtained through international loans sometimes go to enrich individuals instead of being used to pay for the changes needed for the country's development. At the same time, it would be unjust to impose the burden resulting from these irresponsible decisions upon those who did not make them. The gravity of the situation is all the more evident when we consider that "even the payment of interest alone represents a burden for the economy of poor nations, which deprives the authorities of the money necessary for social development, education, health and the establishment of a fund to create jobs".[61]

Corruption

23.   Corruption is often among the causes of crushing public debt, and is therefore a serious problem which needs to be considered carefully. "Respecting no boundaries, [corruption] involves persons, public and private structures of power and the governing elites". It creates a situation which "encourages impunity and the illicit accumulation of money, lack of trust in political institutions, especially the administration of justice and public investments, which are not always transparent, equal for all and effective".[62]

Here I wish to recall what I wrote in the *Message for the 1998 World Day of Peace* — that

[61] *Propositio* 75.
[62] *Propositio* 37.

the plague of corruption needs to be denounced and combatted forcefully by those in authority, with "the generous support of all citizens, sustained by a firm moral conscience".[63] Appropriate supervisory bodies and transparency in economic and financial transactions are helpful and in many cases stop the spread of corruption, the dire consequences of which fall in the main upon the weakest and most marginal members of society. It is also the poor who are the first to suffer as a result of delays and inefficiency, by not being properly defended, because of structural deficiencies, especially when corruption affects the administration of justice itself.

The drug trade

24.   The drug trade and drug use represent a grave threat to the social fabric of American nations. The drug trade "contributes to crime and violence, to the destruction of family life, to the physical and emotional destruction of many individuals and communities, especially among the young. It also undermines the ethical dimension of work and increases the number of people in prison — in a word, it leads to the degradation of the person created in the image of God".[64] This devastating trade also leads to "the ruin of governments and erodes economic security and

---

[63] No. 5: *AAS* 90 (1998), 152.
[64] *Propositio* 38.

the stability of nations".[65] Here we are facing one of the most urgent challenges which many nations around the world need to address: it is in fact a challenge which threatens many features of the human progress achieved in recent times. For some American nations, the production, trafficking and use of drugs are factors which tarnish their international reputation, because they reduce their credibility and render more difficult the cooperation which they seek with other countries and which is so essential nowadays for harmonious social development.

Ecological concern

25. "And God saw that it was good" (*Gen* 1:25). These words from the first chapter of the Book of Genesis reveal the meaning of what God has done. To men and women, the crown of the entire process of creation, the Creator entrusts the care of the earth (cf. *Gen* 2:15). This brings concrete obligations in the area of ecology for every person. Fulfillment of these obligations supposes an openness to a spiritual and ethical perspective capable of overcoming selfish attitudes and "life-styles which lead to the depletion of natural resources".[66]

In this area too, so relevant today, the action of believers is more important than ever. Alongside legislative and governmental bodies, all peo-

[65] *Ibid.*
[66] *Propositio* 36.

ple of good will must work to ensure the effective protection of the environment, understood as a gift from God. How much ecological abuse and destruction there is in many parts of America! It is enough to think of the uncontrolled emission of harmful gases or the dramatic phenomenon of forest fires, sometimes deliberately set by people driven by selfish interest. Devastations such as these could lead to the desertification of many parts of America, with the inevitable consequences of hunger and misery. This is an especially urgent problem in the forests of Amazonia, an immense territory extending into different countries: from Brazil to Guyana, Surinam, Venezuela, Colombia, Ecuador, Peru and Bolivia.[67] This is one of the world's most precious natural regions because of its bio-diversity which makes it vital for the environmental balance of the entire planet.

---

[67] Cf. *ibid.*

CHAPTER III

THE PATH OF CONVERSION

"Repent therefore and be converted" (*Acts* 3:19)

The urgency of the call to conversion

26.   "The time is fulfilled and the kingdom of God is close at hand: repent and believe the Good News" (*Mk* 1:15). These words with which Jesus began his Galilean ministry still echo in the ears of Bishops, priests, deacons, consecrated men and women and the lay faithful throughout America. Both the recent celebration of the fifth centenary of the first evangelization of America and the commemoration of the two thousandth anniversary of the birth of Jesus, the Great Jubilee we are preparing to celebrate, summon everyone alike to a deeper sense of our Christian vocation. The greatness of the Incarnation and gratitude for the gift of the first proclamation of the Gospel in America are an invitation to respond readily to Christ with a more decisive personal conversion and a stimulus to ever more generous fidelity to the Gospel. Christ's call to conversion finds an echo in the words of the Apostle: "It is time now to wake from sleep, be-

cause our salvation is closer than when we first became believers" (*Rom* 13:11). The encounter with the living Jesus impels us to conversion.

In speaking of conversion, the New Testament uses the word *metanoia*, which means a change of mentality. It is not simply a matter of thinking differently in an intellectual sense, but of revising the reasons behind one's actions in the light of the Gospel. In this regard, Saint Paul speaks of "faith working through love" (*Gal* 5:6). This means that true conversion needs to be prepared and nurtured though the prayerful reading of Sacred Scripture and the practice of the Sacraments of Reconciliation and the Eucharist. Conversion leads to fraternal communion, because it enables us to understand that Christ is the head of the Church, his Mystical Body; it urges solidarity, because it makes us aware that whatever we do for others, especially for the poorest, we do for Christ himself. Conversion, therefore, fosters a new life, in which there is no separation between faith and works in our daily response to the universal call to holiness. In order to speak of conversion, the gap between faith and life must be bridged. Where this gap exists, Christians are such only in name. To be true disciples of the Lord, believers must bear witness to their faith, and "witnesses testify not only with words, but also with their lives".[68] We must keep in mind the words of Jesus: "Not every one who

---

[68] SYNOD OF BISHOPS, Second Extraordinary General Assembly, Final Summary *Ecclesia sub Verbo Dei Mysteria Christi*

says to me, 'Lord, Lord!' shall enter the kingdom of heaven, but he who does the will of my Father who is in heaven" (*Mt* 7:21). Openness to the Father's will supposes a total self-giving, including even the gift of one's life: "The greatest witness is martyrdom".[69]

The social dimension of conversion

27. Yet conversion is incomplete if we are not aware of the demands of the Christian life and if we do not strive to meet them. In this regard, the Synod Fathers noted that unfortunately "at both the personal and communal level there are great shortcomings in relation to a more profound conversion and with regard to relationships between sectors, institutions and groups within the Church".[70] "He who does not love his brother whom he has seen, cannot love God whom he has not seen" (*1 Jn* 4:20).

Fraternal charity means attending to all the needs of our neighbor. "If any one has the world's goods and sees his brother in need, yet closes his heart against him, how does God's love abide in him?" (*1 Jn* 3:17). Hence, for the Christian people of America conversion to the Gospel means to revise "all the different areas and aspects of life, especially those related to the social

Celebrans pro Salute Mundi (December 7, 1985), II, B, a, 2: *Enchiridion Vaticanum* 9, 1795.
[69] *Propositio* 30.
[70] *Propositio* 34.

order and the pursuit of the common good".[71] It will be especially necessary "to nurture the growing awareness in society of the dignity of every person and, therefore, to promote in the community a sense of the duty to participate in political life in harmony with the Gospel".[72] Involvement in the political field is clearly part of the vocation and activity of the lay faithful.[73]

In this regard, however, it is most important, especially in a pluralistic society, to understand correctly the relationship between the political community and the Church, and to distinguish clearly between what individual believers or groups of believers undertake in their own name as citizens guided by Christian conscience and what they do in the name of the Church in communion with their Pastors. The Church which, in virtue of her office and competence, can in no way be confused with the political community nor be tied to any political system, is both a sign and safeguard of the transcendent character of the human person.[74]

[71] *Ibid.*

[72] *Ibid.*

[73] Cf. SECOND VATICAN ECUMENICAL COUNCIL, Dogmatic Constitution on the Church *Lumen Gentium*, 31.

[74] Cf. SECOND VATICAN ECUMENICAL COUNCIL, Pastoral Constitution on the Church in the Modern World *Gaudium et Spes*, 76; JOHN PAUL II, Post-Synodal Apostolic Exhortation *Christifideles Laici* (December 30, 1988), 42: *AAS* 81 (1989), 472-476.

28.   In this life, conversion is a goal which is never fully attained: on the path which the disciple is called to follow in the footsteps of Jesus, conversion is a lifelong task. While we are in this world, our intention to repent is always exposed to temptations. Since "no one can serve two masters" (*Mt* 6:24), the change of mentality (*metanoia*) means striving to assimilate the values of the Gospel, which contradict the dominant tendencies of the world. Hence there is a need to renew constantly "the encounter with the living Jesus Christ", since this, as the Synod Fathers pointed out, is the way "which leads us to continuing conversion".[75]

The universal call to conversion has special implications for the Church in America, involved as she is in the renewal of faith. The Synod Fathers expressed this very specific and demanding task in this way: "This conversion demands especially of us Bishops a genuine identification with the personal style of Jesus Christ, who leads us to simplicity, poverty, responsibility for others and the renunciation of our own advantage, so that, like him and not trusting in human means, we may draw from the strength of the Holy Spirit and of the Word all the power of the Gospel, remaining open above all to those who are furthest away and excluded".[76] To be Pastors after

[75] *Propositio* 26.
[76] *Ibid.*

God's own heart (cf. *Jer* 3:15), it is essential to adopt a mode of living which makes us like the one who says of himself: "I am the good shepherd" (*Jn* 10:11), and to whom Saint Paul points when he writes: "Imitate me as I imitate Christ" (*1 Cor* 11:1).

Guided by the Holy Spirit to a new way of living

29.   The proposal of a new style of life applies not only to the Pastors, but to all Christians living in America. They are asked to know more deeply and to make their own a genuine Christian spirituality. "In effect, the term spirituality means a mode or form of life in keeping with Christian demands. Spirituality is 'life in Christ' and 'in the Spirit', which is accepted in faith, expressed in love and inspired by hope, and so becomes the daily life of the Church community".[77] In this sense, by spirituality, which is the goal of conversion, we mean "not a part of life, but the whole of life guided by the Holy Spirit".[78] Among the many elements of spirituality which all Christians must make their own, prayer holds a pre-eminent place. Prayer leads Christians "little by little to acquire a contemplative view of reality, enabling them to recognize God in every moment and in every thing; to contemplate God

[77] *Propositio* 28.
[78] *Ibid.*

in every person; to seek his will in all that happens".[79]

Prayer, both personal and liturgical, is the duty of every Christian. "Jesus Christ, the Good News of the Father, warns us that without him we can do nothing (cf. *Jn* 15:5). He himself, in the decisive moments of his life, before doing something, used to withdraw to an isolated place to give himself to prayer and contemplation, and he asked the Apostles to do the same".[80] He tells his disciples without exception: "Go into your room and shut the door and pray to your Father who is in secret" (*Mt* 6:6). This intense life of prayer must be adapted to the capacity and condition of each Christian, so that in all the different situations of life each one may be able "to drink of the one Spirit (cf. *1 Cor* 12:13) from the wellspring of their encounter with Christ".[81] In this sense, contemplation is not a privilege reserved to the few; on the contrary, in parishes, in communities and movements there is a need to foster a spirituality clearly oriented to contemplation of the fundamental truths of faith: the mysteries of the Trinity, the Incarnation of the Word, the Redemption of humanity, and the other great saving works of God.[82]

Men and women who are dedicated exclusively to the contemplative life accomplish a funda-

[79] *Ibid.*
[80] *Propositio* 27.
[81] *Ibid.*
[82] Cf. *ibid.*

mental mission in the Church in America. As the Second Vatican Council put it, they are "a glory of the Church and a source of heavenly graces".[83] Therefore, the monasteries which exist throughout the continent must be "especially loved by the Pastors, who should be deeply convinced that souls dedicated to the contemplative life obtain an abundance of grace, through the prayer, penance and contemplation to which they have given their lives. Contemplatives must know that they are part of the Church's mission in the present and that, by the witness of their lives, they work for the spiritual good of the faithful, and help them to seek the face of God in everyday life".[84]

Christian spirituality is nourished above all by a constant sacramental life, since the Sacraments are the root and endless source of God's grace which believers need to sustain them on their earthly pilgrimage. The sacramental life needs to be complemented by the values of popular piety, values which will be enriched in turn by sacramental practice and saved from falling into the danger of routine. It should also be noted that this spirituality is not opposed to the social responsibilities of the Christian life. On the contrary, in following the path of prayer, believers become more conscious of the Gospel's demands

[83] Decree on the Renewal of Religious Life *Perfectae Caritatis*, 7. Cf. JOHN PAUL II, Post-Synodal Apostolic Exhortation *Vita Consecrata* (March 25, 1996), 8: *AAS* 88 (1996), 382.
[84] *Propositio* 27.

and of their duties towards others. Through prayer, they are strengthened with the grace they need to persevere in doing good. In order to mature spiritually, Christians do well to seek the counsel of the Church's ministers or of other persons expert in the field of spiritual direction, which is a traditional practice in the Church. The Synod Fathers felt that it was necessary to recommend to priests this important ministry.[85]

The universal call to holiness

30. "Be holy, for I the Lord your God am holy" (*Lev* 19:2). The Special Assembly for America of the Synod of Bishops has wished to offer a forceful reminder to all Christians of the importance of the doctrine of the universal call to holiness in the Church.[86] This is one of the key points of the Second Vatican Council's Dogmatic Constitution on the Church.[87] Conversion is directed to holiness, since conversion "is not an end in itself but a journey towards God who is holy. To be holy is to be like God and to glorify his name in the works which we accomplish in our lives (cf. *Mt* 5:16)".[88] On the path of holiness, Jesus Christ is the point of reference and

---

[85] Cf. *Propositio* 28.

[86] Cf. *Propositio* 29.

[87] Cf. *Lumen Gentium*, Chapter V; SYNOD OF BISHOPS, Second Extraordinary General Assembly, Final Report *Ecclesia sub Verbo Dei Mysteria Christi Celebrans pro Salute Mundi* (December 7, 1985), II, A, 4-5: *Enchiridion Vaticanum* 9, 1791-1793.

[88] *Propositio* 29.

the model to be imitated: he is "the Holy One of God", and was recognized as such (cf. *Mk* 1:24). It is he who teaches us that the heart of holiness is love, which leads even to giving our lives for others (cf. *Jn* 15:13). Therefore, to imitate the holiness of God, as it was made manifest in Jesus Christ his Son, "is nothing other than to extend in history his love, especially towards the poor, the sick and the needy (cf. *Lk* 10:25ff.)".[89]

Jesus, the one way to holiness

31. "I am the Way, the Truth and the Life" (*Jn* 14:6). With these words, Jesus presents himself as the one path which leads to holiness. But a specific knowledge of this way comes chiefly through the word of God which the Church proclaims in her preaching. Therefore, the Church in America "must give a clear priority to prayerful reflection on Sacred Scripture by all the faithful".[90] This reading of the Bible, accompanied by prayer, is known in the tradition of the Church as *lectio divina*, and it is a practice to be encouraged among all Christians. For priests, the *lectio divina* must be a basic feature of the preparation of their homilies, especially the Sunday homily.[91]

[89] *Ibid.*
[90] *Propositio* 32.
[91] Cf. JOHN PAUL II, Apostolic Letter *Dies Domini* (May 31, 1998), 40: *AAS* 90 (1998), 738.

32.   Conversion (*metanoia*), to which every person is called, leads to an acceptance and appropriation of the new vision which the Gospel proposes. This requires leaving behind our worldly way of thinking and acting, which so often heavily conditions our behavior. As Sacred Scripture reminds us, the old man must die and the new man must be born, that is, the whole person must be renewed "in full knowledge after the image of the Creator" (*Col* 3:10). Strongly recommended on this path of conversion and quest for holiness are "the ascetical practices which have always been part of the Church's life and which culminate in the Sacrament of forgiveness, received and celebrated with the right dispositions".[92] Only those reconciled with God can be prime agents of true reconciliation with and among their brothers and sisters.

The present crisis of the Sacrament of Penance, from which the Church in America is not exempt and about which I have voiced my concern from the beginning of my Pontificate,[93] will be overcome by resolute and patient pastoral efforts.

On this point, the Synod Fathers rightly asked "that priests give the necessary time to the Sacrament of Penance, and strongly and insistently invite the faithful to receive the Sacrament,

[92] *Propositio* 33.
[93] Cf. Encyclical Letter *Redemptor Hominis* (March 4, 1979), 20: *AAS* 71 (1979) 309-316.

without the Pastors themselves neglecting frequent confession in their own lives".[94] Bishops and priests personally experience the mysterious encounter with the forgiving Christ in the Sacrament of Penance and they are privileged witnesses of his merciful love.

The Catholic Church, which embraces men and women "of every nation, race, people and tongue" (*Rev* 7:9) is called to be, "in a world marked by ideological, ethnic, economic and cultural divisions", the "living sign of the unity of the human family".[95] In the multiplicity of nations and the variety of ethnic groups, as in the features common to the entire continent, America presents many differences which cannot be ignored and which the Church has the duty to address. Thanks to effective efforts to integrate the members of the People of God within each country and to unite the members of the particular Churches of the various countries, today's differences can be a source of mutual enrichment. As the Synod Fathers rightly affirmed, "it is most important that the Church throughout America be a living sign of reconciled communion, an enduring appeal to solidarity and a witness ever present in our various political, economic and social systems".[96] This is a significant contribution which believers can make to the unity of the American continent.

[94] *Propositio 33.*
[95] *Ibid.*
[96] *Ibid.*

CHAPTER IV

THE PATH TO COMMUNION

"As you, Father, are in me and I in you, may they also be one in us" (*Jn* 17:21)

The Church, sacrament of communion

33.   "Faced with a divided world which is in search of unity, we must proclaim with joy and firm faith that God is communion, Father, Son and Holy Spirit, unity in distinction, and that he calls all people to share in that same Trinitarian communion. We must proclaim that this communion is the magnificent plan of God the Father; that Jesus Christ, the Incarnate Lord, is the heart of this communion, and that the Holy Spirit works ceaselessly to create communion and to restore it when it is broken. We must proclaim that the Church is the sign and instrument of the communion willed by God, begun in time and destined for completion in the fullness of the Kingdom".[97] The Church is the sign of communion because her members, like branches, share

---

[97] *Propositio* 40; cf. SECOND VATICAN ECUMENICAL COUNCIL, Dogmatic Constitution on the Church *Lumen Gentium*, 2.

the life of Christ, the true vine (cf. *Jn* 15:5). Through communion with Christ, Head of the Mystical Body, we enter into living communion with all believers.

This communion, present in the Church and essential to her nature,[98] must be made visible in concrete signs, "such as communal prayer for one another, the desire for closer relations between Episcopal Conferences and between Bishops, fraternal ties between dioceses and parishes, and communication among pastoral workers with a view to specific missionary works".[99] Communion requires that the deposit of faith be preserved in its purity and integrity, together with the unity of the College of Bishops under the authority of the Successor of Peter. In this context, the Synod Fathers stressed that "the strengthening of the Petrine ministry is fundamental for the preservation of the Church's unity", and that "the full exercise of the primacy of Peter is fundamental for the Church's identity and vitality in America".[100] By the Lord's mandate, Peter and his Successors have the task of confirming their brethren in faith (cf. *Lk* 22:32) and of feeding the entire flock of Christ (cf. *Jn* 21:15-17). The Successor of the Prince of the Apostles is called to be the rock upon which the Church is built, and to ex-

[98] Cf. CONGREGATION FOR THE DOCTRINE OF THE FAITH, Letter to the Bishops of the Catholic Church on Some Aspects of the Church Understood as Communion *Communio Notio* (May 28, 1992), Nos. 3-6: *AAS* 85 (1993), 839-841.
[99] *Propositio* 40.
[100] *Ibid.*

ercise the ministry belonging to the one to whom the keys of the Kingdom were given (cf. *Mt* 16:18-19). The Vicar of Christ is in fact "the enduring principle of unity and the visible foundation" of the Church.[101]

Christian initiation and communion

34.   Communion of life in the Church comes through the sacraments of Christian initiation: Baptism, Confirmation and the Eucharist. Baptism is "the doorway to the spiritual life; it makes us members of Christ and draws us into the body of the Church".[102] In Confirmation, the baptized "are joined more completely to the Church, they are enriched with special strength by the Holy Spirit and thus are more solemnly obliged to spread and defend the faith in word and deed as true witnesses of Christ".[103] The journey of Christian initiation comes to completion and reaches its summit in the Eucharist, which fully incorporates the baptized into the Body of Christ.[104]

"These sacraments are an excellent opportunity for an effective evangelization and catechesis,

[101] FIRST VATICAN ECUMENICAL COUNCIL, Dogmatic Constitution on the Church of Christ *Pastor Aeternus*, Prologue: *DS* 3051.

[102] ECUMENICAL COUNCIL OF FLORENCE, Bull of Union *Exultate Deo* (November 22, 1439): *DS* 1314.

[103] SECOND VATICAN ECUMENICAL COUNCIL, Dogmatic Constitution on the Church *Lumen Gentium*, 11.

[104] Cf. SECOND VATICAN ECUMENICAL COUNCIL, Decree on the Ministry and Life of Priests *Presbyterorum Ordinis*, 5.

when preparation for them is entrusted to people of faith and competence".[105] While dioceses in America have made undeniable progress in preparing people for the sacraments of Christian initiation, the Synod Fathers nonetheless expressed regret that "many receive them without adequate formation".[106] In the case of the Baptism of children, efforts to catechize the parents and godparents should not be spared.

The Eucharist as center of communion with God and with each other

35. The Eucharist is more than simply the culmination of Christian initiation. While Baptism and Confirmation serve as a beginning and introduction to the life of the Church and cannot be repeated,[107] the Eucharist is the living and lasting center around which the entire community of the Church gathers.[108] The various aspects of the Eucharist reveal its inexhaustible wealth: it is at one and the same time a Sacrament of Sacrifice, Communion and Presence.[109]

The Eucharist is the outstanding moment of encounter with the living Christ. For this reason, by their preaching and catechesis, the Pastors of

[105] *Propositio* 41.
[106] *Ibid.*
[107] Cf. ECUMENICAL COUNCIL OF TRENT, Session VII, *Decree on the Sacraments*, Canon 9: *DS* 1609.
[108] Cf. SECOND VATICAN ECUMENICAL COUNCIL, Dogmatic Constitution on the Church *Lumen Gentium*, 26.
[109] Cf. JOHN PAUL II, Encyclical Letter *Redemptor Hominis* (March 4, 1979), 20: *AAS* 71 (1979), 309-316.

the People of God in America must strive "to give the Sunday Eucharistic celebration new strength, as the source and summit of the Church's life, the safeguard of communion in the Body of Christ, and an invitation to solidarity, expressing the Lord's command: 'Love one another as I have loved you' (*Jn* 13:34)".[110] As the Synod Fathers suggest, an effort of this kind must include a number of fundamental aspects. First of all, there is a need to renew in the faithful the sense that the Eucharist is an immense gift: this will lead them to do all they can to participate actively and worthily, at least on Sundays and Holy Days. At the same time, "efforts by priests to make attendance possible, even for the most distant communities" must be encouraged.[111] The faithful need to be reminded that "their full, conscious and active participation, although essentially distinct from the office of the ordained priest, is an exercise of the common priesthood received in Baptism".[112]

The need of the faithful to attend the Eucharist and the difficulties that arise from the shortage of priests make clear how urgent it is to promote priestly vocations.[113] The whole Church

---

[110] *Propositio* 42; cf. JOHN PAUL II, Apostolic Letter *Dies Domini* (May 31, 1998), 69: *AAS* 90 (1998), 755-756.

[111] *Propositio* 41.

[112] *Propositio* 42; cf. SECOND VATICAN ECUMENICAL COUNCIL, Constitution on the Sacred Liturgy *Sacrosanctum Concilium*, 14; Dogmatic Constitution on the Church *Lumen Gentium*, 10.

[113] Cf. *Propositio* 42.

in America needs to be reminded also of "the link between the Eucharist and charity",[114] a link which was expressed in the early Church by the joining of the *agape* and the Eucharistic Supper.[115] As a result of the grace received in the Sacrament, sharing in the Eucharist must lead to a more fervent exercise of charity.

The Bishops as builders of communion

36. Precisely because it signifies life, communion in the Church must constantly increase. Therefore, the Bishops, remembering that "each of them is the visible principle and foundation of the unity of his particular Church",[116] cannot but feel duty-bound to promote communion in their dioceses, so that the drive for a new evangelization in America may be more effective. Working in favor of this communion are the structures which the Second Vatican Council called for as a means of supporting the diocesan Bishop's work, and which post-conciliar legislation has spelled out in greater detail.[117] "It is up to the Bishop,

---

[114] *Propositio* 41.

[115] Cf. SECOND VATICAN ECUMENICAL COUNCIL, Decree on the Apostolate of the Laity *Apostolicam Actuositatem*, 8.

[116] SECOND VATICAN ECUMENICAL COUNCIL, Dogmatic Constitution on the Church *Lumen Gentium*, 23.

[117] Decree on the Pastoral Office of Bishops in the Church *Christus Dominus*, 27; Decree on the Ministry and Life of Priests *Presbyterorum Ordinis*, 7; PAUL VI, Motu Proprio *Ecclesiae Sanctae* (August 6, 1966), I, 15-17: *AAS* 58 (1966), 766-767; *Code of Canon Law*, Canons 495, 502, 511; *Code of Canons of the Eastern Churches*, Canons 264, 271, 272.

with the help of the priests, deacons, religious and lay people to implement a coordinated pastoral plan, which is systematic and participatory, involving all the members of the Church and awakening in them a missionary consciousness".[118]

Each Ordinary will make sure to promote among priests and lay faithful the sense that the diocese is the visible expression of the Church's communion, which is formed at the table of the Word and of the Eucharist, around the Bishop in union with the College of Bishops and under its head, the Roman Pontiff. As a particular Church, the diocese is charged with initiating and deepening the encounter of all the members of God's People with Jesus Christ,[119] respecting and fostering that plurality and diversivification which are not obstacles to unity but which give it the character of communion.[120] The spirit of participation and shared responsibility in the working of diocesan structures will certainly be strengthened if the nature of the particular Church is better known and appreciated.[121]

Deeper communion between the particular Churches

37. The Special Assembly for America of the Synod of Bishops was the first ever to have gath-

---

[118] *Propositio* 43.

[119] Cf. *Propositio* 45.

[120] Cf. CONGREGATION FOR THE DOCTRINE OF THE FAITH, Letter to the Bishops of the Catholic Church on Some Aspects of the Church Understood as Communion *Communio Notio* (May 28, 1992), Nos. 15-16: *AAS* 85 (1993), 847-848.

[121] Cf. *ibid.*

ered Bishops from the entire continent, and it was seen by all as a special grace of the Lord to the pilgrim Church in America. It strengthened the communion which must exist among the ecclesial communities of the continent, making clear to all the need for this communion to grow. Experiences of episcopal communion, more frequent since the Second Vatican Council as a result of the growth of Bishops' Conferences, should be seen as encounters with the living Christ, present in the brothers gathered in his name (cf. *Mt* 18:20).

The experience of the Synod showed just as clearly the value of a communion transcending individual Conferences of Bishops. Even though structures for dialogue between Conferences already exist, the Synod Fathers underlined the benefit of inter-American gatherings, such as those sponsored by the Episcopal Conferences of various American countries, as an expression of practical solidarity and a chance to study common challenges to evangelization in America.[122] It would be helpful to specify more exactly the nature of these meetings, so that they may become a better expression of communion among all Bishops. Beyond these more inclusive meetings, it could be useful, whenever circumstances require it, to establish special commissions to explore more deeply issues which concern America as a whole. Areas in which it seems especially neces-

[122] Cf. *Propositio* 44.

sary "to strengthen cooperation are the sharing of information on pastoral matters, missionary collaboration, education, immigration and ecumenism".[123]

The Bishops, whose duty it is to promote communion among the particular Churches, should encourage the faithful to live this communion more and more, and to assume the "responsibility of developing bonds of communion with the local Churches in other areas of America through education, the exchange of information, fraternal ties between parishes and dioceses, and projects involving cooperation and joint intervention in questions of greater importance, especially those affecting the poor".[124]

Fraternal communion
with the Eastern Catholic Churches

38.   The recent phenomenon of the establishment and development in America of Eastern Catholic particular Churches, with their own hierarchy, was a matter of special attention on the part of some Synod Fathers. A genuine desire to embrace, in ways both cordial and practical, these brethren in the faith and in hierarchical communion under the Successor of Peter led the Synod to propose concrete ways for the particular Churches of the Latin rite to offer fraternal assistance to the Eastern Catholic Churches

[123] *Ibid.*
[124] *Ibid.*

throughout the continent. Thus, for example, the possibility was raised that Latin rite priests, especially those with Eastern roots, might offer liturgical assistance to Eastern communities which do not have enough priests of their own. Likewise, with regard to sacred buildings, the Eastern faithful could use Latin rite Churches wherever this seems appropriate.

In this spirit of communion, it is worth considering a few proposals of the Synod Fathers: namely, that — where necessary — mixed commissions charged with studying common pastoral problems be created in national Episcopal Conferences and in international agencies for cooperation among Bishops; that catechesis and theological formation for lay people and seminarians of the Latin Church include knowledge of the living tradition of the Christian East; that the Bishops of the Eastern Catholic Churches participate in the Latin Episcopal Conferences of the different countries.[125] This fraternal cooperation, while offering valuable help to the Eastern Churches of recent foundation in America, will certainly also enrich the particular Churches of the Latin rite with the spiritual heritage of the Eastern Christian tradition.

The priesthood as a sign of unity

39. "As a member of a particular Church, each priest must be a sign of communion with

[125] Cf. *Propositio* 60.

the Bishop, since he is his immediate collaborator, in union with his brothers in the priesthood. With pastoral charity, he exercises his ministry, chiefly in the community entrusted to him, and he leads his community to encounter Christ the Good Shepherd. His vocation requires him to be a sign of unity. Therefore, he must avoid any involvement in party politics, since this would divide the community".[126] The Synod Fathers call for "a pastoral plan for diocesan clergy, to strengthen their spirituality and their sense of mission and identity, centered on following Christ, the eternal High Priest, always striving to obey the Father's will. Christ is the model of generous dedication, of austerity of life and of service even unto death. The priest should be conscious of the fact that, by virtue of the Sacrament of Orders, he is the bearer of grace, which he communicates to his brothers and sisters in the sacraments. He himself is sanctified in the exercise of his ministry".[127]

The field in which priests work is vast. Therefore they should concentrate on what is essential to their ministry: "letting themselves be configured to Christ the Head and Shepherd, the source of all pastoral charity, offering themselves each day with Christ in the Eucharist, in order to help the faithful both personally and commu-

---

[126] *Propositio* 49.
[127] *Ibid.*

nally to experience the living Jesus Christ".[128] As witnesses and disciples of the merciful Christ, they are called to be instruments of forgiveness and reconciliation, putting themselves generously at the service of the faithful in the spirit of the Gospel.

As pastors of the People of God in America, priests must also be alert to the challenges of the world today and sensitive to the problems and hopes of their people, sharing their experiences and growing, above all, in solidarity towards the poor. They should be careful to discern the charisms and strengths of the faithful who might be leaders in the community, listening to them and through dialogue encouraging their participation and co-responsibility. This will lead to a better distribution of tasks, enabling priests "to dedicate themselves to what is most closely tied to the encounter with and the proclamation of Jesus Christ, and thus to represent better within the community the presence of Jesus who draws his people together".[129]

The task of discerning charisms also includes knowing how best to use those priests who show an aptitude for special ministries. Moreover, every priest is expected to offer his fraternal help to other priests and to turn trustingly to them in time of need.

[128] *Ibid.*; cf. SECOND VATICAN ECUMENICAL COUNCIL, Decree on the Ministry and Life of Priests *Presbyterorum Ordinis*, 14.
[129] *Propositio* 49.

Given the outstanding number of priests in America who, by God's grace, strive to meet the challenges of a truly remarkable workload, I join the Synod Fathers in acknowledging and praising their "untiring commitment as pastors, preachers of the Gospel and agents of ecclesial communion, in thanking them and in encouraging them to continue to offer their lives in service of the Gospel".[130]

Promoting vocations

40. The indispensable role of the priest within the community must lead all the members of the Church in America to recognize the importance of promoting vocations. The American continent has many young people, who represent an immense spiritual resource. Therefore, it is necessary to foster vocations to the priesthood and religious life where they first develop, and Christian families must be invited to support their children if they feel called to follow this path.[131] Vocations "are a gift of God" and "they are born in communities of faith, above all in the family, the parish, Catholic schools and other Church organizations. Bishops and priests are particularly responsible for encouraging vocations by personally presenting the call, and above all by their witness of a life of fidelity, joy, enthusiasm and holiness. The entire People of God is responsible for pro-

[130] *Ibid.*
[131] Cf. *Propositio* 51.

moting vocations, and does so chiefly by persistent and humble prayer for vocations".[132]

As places which accept and train those called to the priesthood, seminaries must prepare the future ministers of the Church to live "a solid spirituality of communion with Christ the Shepherd and of openness to the workings of the Spirit, that will make them specially able to discern the needs of God's People and their various charisms, and to work together".[133] Therefore, in seminaries "there should be special insistence upon specifically spiritual formation, so that through constant conversion, the spirit of prayer, the practice of the Sacraments of the Eucharist and Penance, the candidates may learn to be close to the Lord and learn to commit themselves generously to pastoral work".[134] Those responsible for formation should carefully supervise and guide the seminarians towards emotional maturity so that they may be fit to embrace priestly celibacy and be prepared to live in communion with their brother priests. They should also foster in seminarians the capacity for critical observation so that they can discern true and false values, since this is an essential requirement for establishing a constructive dialogue with the world of today.

Special attention needs to be given to vocations among indigenous peoples: they need a formation which takes account of their culture.

[132] *Propositio* 48.
[133] *Propositio* 51.
[134] *Propositio* 52.

While receiving a proper theological and pastoral formation for their future ministry, these candidates for the priesthood should not be uprooted from their own culture.[135]

The Synod Fathers wished to thank and bless all those who devote their lives to the formation of future priests in seminaries. They also invited the Bishops to assign the most suitable priests to this work, after preparing them with specific training for this delicate mission.[136]

Renewing parishes

41.   The parish is a privileged place where the faithful concretely experience the Church.[137] Today in America as elsewhere in the world the parish is facing certain difficulties in fulfilling its mission. The parish needs to be constantly renewed on the basis of the principle that "the parish must continue to be above all a Eucharistic community"[138] This principle implies that "parishes are called to be welcoming and fraternal, places of Christian initiation, of education in and celebration of the faith, open to the full range of charisms, services and ministries, organized in a communal and responsible way, capable of utilizing existing movements of the apostolate, attentive to the cultural diversity of the people, open

[135] Cf. *ibid.*
[136] Cf. *ibid.*
[137] Cf. *Propositio* 46.
[138] *Ibid.*

to pastoral projects which go beyond the individual parish, and alert to the world in which they live".[139]

Because of the particular problems they present, special attention needs to be given to parishes in large urban areas, where the difficulties are such that normal parish structures are inadequate and the opportunities for the apostolate are significantly reduced. The institution of the parish, however, retains its importance and needs to be preserved. For this, there is a need "to keep looking for ways in which the parish and its pastoral structures can be more effective in urban areas".[140] One way of renewing parishes, especially urgent for parishes in large cities, might be to consider the parish as a community of communities and movements.[141] It seems timely therefore to form ecclesial communities and groups of a size that allows for true human relationships. This will make it possible to live communion more intensely, ensuring that it is fostered not only "ad intra", but also with the parish communities to which such groups belong, and with the entire diocesan and universal Church. In such a human context, it will be easier to gather to hear the word of God, to reflect on the range of human problems in the light of

[139] *Ibid.*

[140] *Propositio 35.*

[141] Cf. FOURTH GENERAL CONFERENCE OF THE LATIN AMERICAN BISHOPS, Santo Domingo, October 1992: *New Evangelization, Human Promotion and Christian Culture,* 58.

70

this word, and gradually to make responsible decisions inspired by the all-embracing love of Christ.[142] The institution of the parish, thus renewed, "can be the source of great hope. It can gather people in community, assist family life, overcome the sense of anonymity, welcome people and help them to be involved in their neighborhood and in society".[143] In this way, every parish, and especially city parishes, can promote nowadays a more person-centered evangelization and better cooperate with other social, educational and community work.[144]

Moreover, "this kind of renewed parish needs as its leader a pastor who has a deep experience of the living Christ, a missionary spirit, a father's heart, who is capable of fostering spiritual life, preaching the Gospel and promoting cooperation. A renewed parish needs the collaboration of lay people and therefore a director of pastoral activity and a pastor who is able to work with others. Parishes in America should be distinguished by their missionary spirit, which leads them to reach out to those who are faraway".[145]

Permanent deacons

42. For serious pastoral and theological reasons, the Second Vatican Council decided to re-

[142] Cf. JOHN PAUL II, Encyclical Letter *Redemptoris Missio* (December 7, 1990), 51: *AAS* 83 (1991), 298-299.

[143] *Propositio* 35.

[144] Cf. *Propositio* 46.

[145] *Ibid.*

store the diaconate as a permanent element of the hierarchy of the Latin Church, leaving to the Episcopal Conferences, with the approval of the Supreme Pontiff, the task of assessing whether and where to establish permanent deacons.[146] The experience has varied significantly, not only in the different parts of America but even between dioceses of the same area. "Some dioceses have trained and ordained a good number of deacons, and they are fully satisfied with their integration and their ministry".[147] Here we see with joy how deacons "sustained by the grace of the Sacrament, in the ministry (*diakonia*) of the Liturgy, of the word and of charity are at the service of the People of God, in communion with the Bishop and his priests".[148] Other dioceses have not followed this path, while elsewhere there have been difficulties in integrating permanent deacons into the hierarchical structure.

With due respect for the freedom of the particular Churches to restore the permanent diaconate, with the approval of the Supreme Pontiff, it is clear that for such a move to be successful there has to be a careful selection process, solid formation and continuous attention to the suitability of the candidates, as well as constant con-

---

[146] Cf. Dogmatic Constitution on the Church *Lumen Gentium*, 29; PAUL VI, Motu Proprio *Sacrum Diaconatus Ordinem* (June 18, 1967), I, 1: *AAS* 59 (1967), 699.

[147] *Propositio* 50.

[148] SECOND VATICAN ECUMENICAL COUNCIL, Dogmatic Constitution on the Church *Lumen Gentium*, 29.

cern for them once they are ordained, and — in the case of married deacons — concern as well for their families, wives and children.[149]

Consecrated life

43. The history of evangelization in America bears eloquent testimony to the missionary work accomplished by countless consecrated Religious who from the beginning proclaimed the Gospel, defended the rights of the indigenous peoples and, with heroic love for Christ, dedicated themselves to service of the People of God on the continent.[150] The contribution of Religious to the proclamation of the Gospel in America is still enormously important; it is a varied contribution shaped by the charisms of each group: "Institutes of contemplative life which witness to God as absolute; apostolic and missionary Institutes which make Christ present in all the many different areas of human life; Secular Institutes which help to resolve the tension between real openness to the values of the modern world and the profound offering of one's heart to God. New Institutes and new forms of consecrated life are also coming into being, and these require evangelical discernment".[151]

[149] Cf. *Propositio* 50; CONGREGATION FOR CATHOLIC EDUCATION and CONGREGATION FOR THE CLERGY, *Ratio Fundamentalis Institutionis Diaconorum Permanentium* and *Directorium pro Ministerio et Vita Diaconorum Permanentium* (February 22, 1998), *AAS* 90 (1998): 843-926.

[150] Cf. *Propositio* 53.

[151] *Ibid.*; cf. THIRD GENERAL CONFERENCE OF THE LATIN AMERICAN BISHOPS, Puebla 1979, *Message to the Peoples of Latin America*, No. 775.

Since "the future of the new evangelization . . . is unthinkable without the renewed contribution of women, especially women Religious",[152] it is urgent to promote their participation in the various areas of Church life, including decision-making processes, especially on issues which concern them directly.[153]

"Today too the witness of a life consecrated completely to God is an eloquent proclamation of the fact that God suffices to give fulfillment to the life of each person".[154] This consecration to the Lord must become generous service in the spreading of God's Kingdom. For this reason, on the threshold of the Third Millennium, it is necessary to ensure "that consecrated life be more highly esteemed and promoted by Bishops, priests, and Christian communities, and that, conscious of the joy and responsibility of their vocation, consecrated religious be fully integrated into the particular Church to which they belong, fostering communion and mutual cooperation".[155]

Lay faithful and the renewal of the Church

44. "The teaching of the Second Vatican Council on the unity of the Church as the Peo-

---

[152] JOHN PAUL II, Post-Synodal Apostolic Exhortation *Vita Consecrata* (March 25, 1996), 57: *AAS* 88 (1996), 429-430.
[153] Cf. *ibid.*, 58, *loc. cit.*, 430.
[154] *Propositio* 53.
[155] *Ibid.*

ple of God gathered into the unity of the Father and the Son and the Holy Spirit stresses that Baptism confers upon all who receive it a dignity which includes the imitation and following of Christ, communion with one another and the missionary mandate".[156] The lay faithful should thus be conscious of their baptismal dignity. For their part, Pastors should have a profound respect "for the witness and evangelizing work of lay people who, incorporated into the People of God through a spirituality of communion, lead their brothers and sisters to encounter the living Jesus Christ. The renewal of the Church in America will not be possible without the active presence of the laity. Therefore, they are largely responsible for the future of the Church".[157]

There are two areas in which lay people live their vocation. The first, and the one best suited to their lay state, is the secular world, which they are called to shape according to God's will.[158] "Their specific activity brings the Gospel to the structures of the world; 'working in holiness wherever they are, they consecrate the world itself to God'".[159] Thanks to the lay faithful, "the presence and mission of the Church in the world is realized in a special way in the variety of

[156] *Propositio* 54.

[157] *Ibid.*

[158] Cf. SECOND VATICAN ECUMENICAL COUNCIL, Dogmatic Constitution on the Church *Lumen Gentium*, 31.

[159] *Propositio* 55; cf. SECOND VATICAN ECUMENICAL COUNCIL, Dogmatic Constitution on the Church *Lumen Gentium*, 34.

charisms and ministries which belong to the laity. Secularity is the true and distinctive mark of the lay person and of lay spirituality, which means that the laity strive to evangelize the various sectors of family, social, professional, cultural and political life. On a continent marked by competition and aggressiveness, unbridled consumerism and corruption, lay people are called to embody deeply evangelical values such as mercy, forgiveness, honesty, transparency of heart and patience in difficult situations. What is expected from the laity is a great creative effort in activities and works demonstrating a life in harmony with the Gospel".[160]

America needs lay Christians able to assume roles of leadership in society. It is urgent to train men and women who, in keeping with their vocation, can influence public life, and direct it to the common good. In political life, understood in its truest and noblest sense as the administration of the common good, they can find the path of their own sanctification. For this, they must be formed in the truths and values of the Church's social teaching, and in the basic notions of a theology of the laity. A deeper knowledge of Christian ethical principles and moral values will enable them to be exponents of these in their own particular setting, proclaiming them even where

---

[160] *Propositio* 55.

appeals are made to the so-called "neutrality of the State".[161]

There is a second area in which many lay faithful are called to work, and this can be called "intra-ecclesial". A good number of lay people in America legitimately aspire to contribute their talents and charisms "to the building of the ecclesial community as delegates of the word, catechists, visitors to the sick and the imprisoned, group leaders, etc." [162] The Synod Fathers expressed the hope that the Church would recognize some of these works as lay ministries, with a basis in the Sacraments of Baptism and Confirmation, without compromising the specific ministries proper to the Sacrament of Orders. This is a large and complex issue and some time ago I established a Commission to study it; [163] in this regard the offices of the Holy See have from time to time provided guidelines.[164] There is a need to promote positive cooperation by properly trained lay men and women in different activities within the Church, while avoiding any confusion with the ordained ministries and the activities proper to the Sacrament of Orders, so that the common priesthood of the faithful remains clearly distinguished from that of the ordained.

[161] Cf. *ibid*.

[162] *Propositio 56*.

[163] Cf. Post-Synodal Apostolic Exhortation *Christifideles Laici* (December 30, 1988), 23: *AAS* 81 (1989), 429-433.

[164] Cf. CONGREGATION FOR THE CLERGY ET AL., Instruction *Ecclesiae de Mysterio* (August 15, 1997): *AAS* 89 (1997), 852-877.

In this respect, the Synod Fathers recommended that the works entrusted to lay people be clearly "distinct from those which constitute steps on the way to the ordained ministry" [165] and which are carried out by candidates for the priesthood before ordination. It was also noted that these lay works "should be undertaken only by men and women who have received the necessary training in accordance with clearly defined criteria: a stable presence, a real readiness to serve a determined group of persons, and the duty of accountability to their Pastor".[166] In any event, while the intra-ecclesial apostolate of lay people needs to be promoted, care must be taken to ensure that it goes hand in hand with the activity proper to the laity, in which their place cannot be taken by priests: the area of temporal realities.

The dignity of women

45.   Particular attention needs to be given to the vocation of women. On other occasions I have expressed my esteem for the specific contribution of women to the progress of humanity and recognized the legitimacy of their aspiration to take part fully in ecclesial, cultural, social and economic life.[167] Without this contribution, we

[165] *Propositio* 56.
[166] *Ibid.*
[167] Cf. Apostolic Letter *Mulieris Dignitatem* (August 15, 1988): *AAS* 80 (1988), 1653-1729; *Letter to Women* (June 29, 1995): *AAS* 87 (1995), 803-812; *Propositio* 11.

would miss the enrichment which only the "feminine genius" [168] can bring to the life of the Church and to society. To fail to recognize this would be an historic injustice, especially in America, if we consider the contribution which women have made to the material and cultural development of the continent, just as they have in handing down and preserving the faith. Indeed, "their role was decisive, above all in consecrated life, in education and in health care". [169]

Unfortunately, in many parts of America women still meet forms of discrimination. It can be said that the face of the poor in America is also the face of many women. That is why the Synod Fathers spoke of a "feminine side of poverty". [170] The Church feels the duty to defend the human dignity which belongs to every person, and "denounces discrimination, sexual abuse and male domination as actions contrary to God's plan". [171] In particular, the Church deplores the appalling practice, sometimes part of a larger plan, of the sterilization of women, especially the poorest and most marginalized, often carried out surreptitiously, without the women themselves realizing it. This is all the more serious when it is done in order to obtain economic aid at the international level.

[168] Apostolic Letter *Mulieris Dignitatem* (August 15, 1988), 31: *AAS* 80 (1988), 1728.
[169] *Propositio* 11.
[170] *Ibid.*
[171] *Ibid.*

The Church throughout America feels committed to show greater concern for women and to defend them "so that society in America can better support family life based on marriage, better protect motherhood and show greater respect for the dignity of all women".[172] There is a need to help women in America to take an active and responsible role in the Church's life and mission,[173] and also to acknowledge the need for the wisdom and cooperation of women in leadership roles within American society.

Challenges facing Christian families

46.   "God the Creator, by forming the first man and woman and commanding them to 'be fruitful and multiply' (*Gen* 1:28), definitively established the family. In this sanctuary life is born and is welcomed as God's gift. The word of God, faithfully read in the family, gradually builds it up as a domestic church and makes it fruitful in human and Christian virtues; it is there that the source of vocations is to be found. Marian devotion, nourished by prayer, will keep families united and prayerful with Mary, like the disciples of Jesus before Pentecost (cf. *Acts* 1:14)".[174] Many insidious forces are endangering the solidity of the institution of the family in most coun-

[172] *Ibid.*
[173] Cf. Post-Synodal Apostolic Exhortation *Christifideles Laici* (December 30, 1988), 49: *AAS* 81 (1989), 486-489.
[174] *Propositio* 12.

tries of America, and these represent so many challenges for Christians. Among them we should mention the increase in divorce, the spread of abortion, infanticide and the contraceptive mentality. Faced with this situation, we need to reaffirm "that the foundation of human life is the conjugal relationship between husband and wife, a relationship which, between Christians, is sacramental".[175]

Hence there is urgent need of a broad catechetical effort regarding the Christian ideal of conjugal communion and family life, including a spirituality of fatherhood and motherhood. Greater pastoral attention must be given to the role of men as husbands and fathers, as well as to the responsibility which they share with their wives for their marriage, the family and the raising of their children. Also required is a serious preparation of young people for marriage, one which clearly presents Catholic teaching on this sacrament at the theological, anthropological and spiritual levels. On a continent like America, characterized by significant population growth, there needs to be a constant increase of pastoral initiatives directed to families.

In order to be a true "domestic church"[176] the Christian family needs to be a setting in which parents hand down the faith, since they are "for their children, by word and example,

[175] *Ibid.*

[176] SECOND VATICAN ECUMENICAL COUNCIL, Dogmatic Constitution on the Church *Lumen Gentium*, 11.

the first heralds of the faith".[177] Families should not fail to set time aside for prayer, in which spouses are united with each other and with their children. There is a need to encourage shared spiritual moments such as participating in the Eucharist on Sundays and Holy Days, receiving the Sacrament of Reconciliation, daily prayer in the family and practical signs of charity. This will strengthen fidelity in marriage and unity in families. In such a family setting it will not be difficult for children to discover a vocation of service in the community and the Church, and to learn, especially by seeing the example of their parents, that family life is a way to realize the universal call to holiness.[178]

Young people, the hope of the future

47.   Young people are a great force in society and for evangelization. They "represent quite a large part of the population in many nations of America. On their encounter with the living Christ depends the hope and expectation of a future of greater communion and solidarity for the Church and society in America".[179] The particular Churches throughout the continent are clearly making real efforts to catechize young people before Confirmation and to offer them other kinds of support in developing their relationship with

[177] *Ibid.*
[178] Cf. *Propositio* 12.
[179] *Propositio* 14.

Christ and their knowledge of the Gospel. The formation process for young people must be constant and active, capable of helping them to find their place in the Church and in the world. Consequently, youth ministry must be one of the primary concerns of Pastors and communities.

In fact, while many young people in America are searching for true meaning in life and are thirsting for God, quite often they lack the conditions needed to take advantage of their abilities and realize their aspirations. Unfortunately, unemployment and the lack of prospects for the future lead them at times to withdrawal and to violence. The resulting sense of frustration not infrequently leads them to abandon the search for God. Faced with this complex situation, "the Church is committed to maintaining her pastoral and missionary commitment to young people, so that they will encounter today the living Jesus Christ".[180]

In her pastoral activity the Church reaches a great number of adolescents and young people through programs for Christian families, catechesis, Catholic educational institutions and community life in parishes. But there are many others, especially among those affected by various kinds of poverty, who remain outside the range of the Church's activity. Young Christians, trained to have a mature missionary consciousness, must become apostles to their contemporaries. There is need for pastoral outreach to young people wher-

[180] *Ibid.*

ever they are found: in schools, universities, the workplace, the countryside, with appropriate adaptation to their particular inclinations. At the parish and diocesan level it would be helpful also to develop a pastoral outreach that takes account of the changing world of young people. Such an effort should seek to engage them in dialogue, take advantage of favorable occasions for meetings on a larger scale, encourage local initiatives and make the most of programs already in place at the interdiocesan and international levels.

And what of those young people who do not grow out of their adolescent attitudes and find it difficult to take on serious and lasting responsibilities? In response to this lack of maturity, young people need to be invited to have courage and they need to be trained to appreciate the value of life-long commitments such as the priesthood, consecrated life and Christian married life.[181]

Leading children to encounter Christ

48. Children are God's gift and a sign of his presence. "There is a need to accompany children in their encounter with Christ, from Baptism to First Communion, since they are part of the living community of faith, hope and love".[182] The Church is grateful for the efforts of parents, teachers, pastoral, social and health care workers, and all those who seek to serve the family and

---

[181] Cf. *ibid.*
[182] *Propositio* 15.

children with the same attitude as Jesus Christ who said: "Let the children come to me, and do not hinder them; for to such belongs the kingdom of heaven" (*Mt* 19:4).

The Synod Fathers rightly deplored and condemned the painful condition of many children throughout America who are denied their dignity, their innocence and even their life. "This condition includes violence, poverty, homelessness, lack of adequate health care and education, the harm inflicted by drugs and alcohol, and other states of neglect and abuse".[183] In this regard, special mention was made during the Synod of the problem of the sexual abuse of children and child prostitution, and the Fathers made an urgent appeal "to all those holding authority in society, that, as a priority, they do all in their power to alleviate the suffering of children in America".[184]

Elements of communion with other Christian Churches and Ecclesial Communities

49.   Between the Catholic Church and the other Christian Churches and Ecclesial Communities there exists a drive towards communion rooted in the Baptism which each administers.[185] It is a drive nourished by prayer, dialogue and joint action. The Synod Fathers wished to express their

[183] *Ibid.*
[184] *Ibid.*
[185] Cf. SECOND VATICAN ECUMENICAL COUNCIL, Decree on Ecumenism *Unitatis Redintegratio*, 3.

special desire "to cooperate in the dialogue already under way with the Orthodox Church, with which we share many elements of faith, sacramental life and piety".[186] The specific proposals of the Synodal assembly concerning non-Catholic Christian Churches and Ecclesial Communities as a whole were numerous. It was suggested in the first place "that Catholic Christians, Pastors and faithful foster cooperation between Christians of the different confessions, in the name of the Gospel, in response to the cry of the poor, by the promotion of justice, by common prayer for unity and by sharing in the word of God and the experience of faith in the living Christ".[187] Also to be promoted, when possible and appropriate, are meetings of experts from the different Churches and Ecclesial Communities aimed at facilitating ecumenical dialogue. Ecumenism should be a subject of reflection and shared experience between the different Catholic Episcopal Conferences in America.

Although the Second Vatican Council refers to all those who are baptized and believe in Christ as "brothers and sisters in the Lord",[188] it is necessary to distinguish clearly between Christian communities, with which ecumenical relations can be established, and sects, cults and other pseudo-religious movements.

[186] *Propositio* 61.
[187] *Ibid.*
[188] Decree on Ecumenism *Unitatis Redintegratio*, 3.

The Church's relations with Jewish communities

50. American society also includes Jewish communities, with which the Church has fostered increasing cooperation in recent years.[189] The history of salvation makes clear our special relationship with the Jewish people. Jesus belongs to the Jewish people and he inaugurated his Church within the Jewish nation. A great part of the Holy Scriptures, which we Christians read as the word of God, constitute a spiritual patrimony which we share with Jews.[190] Consequently any negative attitude in their regard must be avoided, since "in order to be a blessing for the world, Jews and Christians need first to be a blessing for each other".[191]

Non-Christian religions

51. As for non-Christian religions, the Catholic Church rejects nothing in them which is true and holy.[192] Hence, with regard to other religions Catholics intend to emphasize elements of truth wherever they are to be found, while at the same time firmly bearing witness to the newness of the revelation of Christ, preserved in its fullness by

[189] Cf. *Propositio* 62.

[190] Cf. SYNOD OF BISHOPS, Special Assembly for Europe, Declaration *Ut Testes Simus Christi Qui Nos Liberavit* (December 13, 1991), III, 8: *Enchiridion Vaticanum* 13, 653-655.

[191] *Propositio* 62.

[192] Cf. SECOND VATICAN ECUMENICAL COUNCIL, Declaration on the Church's Relation to Non-Christian Religions *Nostra Aetate*, 2.

the Church.[193] Consistent with this attitude, they reject as alien to the spirit of Christ any discrimination or persecution directed against persons on the basis of race, color, condition of life or religion. Difference of religion must never be a cause of violence or war. Instead persons of different beliefs must feel themselves drawn, precisely because of these beliefs, to work together for peace and justice.

"Muslims, like Christians and Jews, call Abraham their father. Consequently throughout America these three communities should live in harmony and work together for the common good. The Church in America must also work for greater mutual respect and good relations with the native American religions".[194] A similar attitude should be fostered with regard to the followers of Hinduism, Buddhism and other religions who have come to America as a result of recent waves of immigration from the East.

---

[193] Cf. *Propositio* 63.
[194] *Ibid.*

CHAPTER V

THE PATH TO SOLIDARITY

"By this all will know that you are my disciples, if you have love for one another" (*Jn* 13:35)

Solidarity, the fruit of communion

52.   "Truly, I say to you, as you did it to one of the least of these my brethren, you did it to me" (*Mt* 25:40; cf. 25:45). The awareness of communion with Christ and with our brothers and sisters, for its part the fruit of conversion, leads to the service of our neighbors in all their needs, material and spiritual, since the face of Christ shines forth in every human being. "Solidarity is thus the fruit of the communion which is grounded in the mystery of the triune God, and in the Son of God who took flesh and died for all. It is expressed in Christian love which seeks the good of others, especially of those most in need".[195]

For the particular Churches of the American continent, this is the source of a commitment to reciprocal solidarity and the sharing of the spir-

[195] *Propositio* 67.

89

itual gifts and material goods with which God has blessed them, fostering in individuals a readiness to work where they are needed. Taking the Gospel as its starting-point, a culture of solidarity needs to be promoted, capable of inspiring timely initiatives in support of the poor and the outcast, especially refugees forced to leave their villages and lands in order to flee violence. The Church in America must encourage the international agencies of the continent to establish an economic order dominated not only by the profit motive but also by the pursuit of the common good of nations and of the international community, the equitable distribution of goods and the integral development of peoples.[196]

The Church's teaching, a statement of the demands of conversion

53.   At a time when in the sphere of morality there is a disturbing spread of relativism and subjectivism, the Church in America is called to proclaim with renewed vigor that conversion consists in commitment to the person of Jesus Christ, with all the theological and moral implications taught by the Magisterium of the Church. There is a need to recognize "the role played by theologians, catechists and religion teachers who, by setting forth the Church's teaching in fidelity to the Magisterium, cooperate directly in the cor-

[196] Cf. *ibid.*

rect formation of the consciences of the faithful".[197] If we believe that Jesus is the Truth (cf. *Jn* 14:6), we cannot fail to desire ardently to be his witnesses in order to bring our brothers and sisters closer to the full truth that dwells in the Son of God made man, who died and rose from the dead for the salvation of the human race. "In this way we will be able to be, in this world, living beacons of faith, hope and charity".[198]

The Church's social doctrine

54. Faced with the grave social problems which, with different characteristics, are present throughout America, Catholics know that they can find in the Church's social doctrine an answer which serves as a starting-point in the search for practical solutions. Spreading this doctrine is an authentic pastoral priority. It is therefore important "that in America the agents of evangelization (Bishops, priests, teachers, pastoral workers, etc.) make their own this treasure which is the Church's social teaching and, inspired by it, become capable of interpreting the present situation and determine the actions to take".[199] In this regard, special care must be taken to train lay persons capable of working, on the basis of their faith in Christ, to transform earthly realities. In addition, it will help to promote and support

[197] *Propositio* 68.
[198] *Ibid.*
[199] *Propositio* 69.

the study of this doctrine in every area of the life of the particular Churches in America, especially in the universities, so that it may be more deeply known and applied to American society. The complex social reality of the continent is a fruitful field for the analysis and application of the universal principles contained in this doctrine.

To this end, it would be very useful to have a compendium or approved synthesis of Catholic social doctrine, including a "Catechism", which would show the connection between it and the new evangelization. The part which the *Catechism of the Catholic Church* devotes to this material, in its treatment of the seventh commandment of the Decalogue, could serve as the starting-point for such a "Catechism of Catholic Social Doctrine". Naturally, as in the case of the *Catechism of the Catholic Church*, such a synthesis would only formulate general principles, leaving their application to further treatment of the specific issues bound up with the different local situations.[200]

An important place in the Church's social doctrine belongs to the right to dignified labor. Consequently, given the high rates of unemployment found in numerous countries in America and the harsh conditions in which many industrial and rural workers find themselves, "it is neces-

---

[200] Cf. SYNOD OF BISHOPS, Second Extraordinary General Assembly, Final Report *Ecclesia sub Verbo Dei Mysteria Christi Celebrans pro Salute Mundi* (December 7, 1985), II, B, a, 4: *Enchiridion Vaticanum* 9, 1797; JOHN PAUL II, Apostolic Constitution *Fidei Depositum* (October 11, 1992): *AAS* 86 (1994), 117; *Catechism of the Catholic Church*, 24.

sary to value work as a factor of the fulfillment and dignity of the human person. It is the ethical responsibility of an organized society to promote and support a culture of work".[201]

The globalization of solidarity

55.   As I mentioned earlier, the complex phenomenon of globalization is one of the features of the contemporary world particularly visible in America. An important part of this many-faceted reality is the economic aspect. By her social doctrine the Church makes an effective contribution to the issues presented by the current globalized economy. Her moral vision in this area "rests on the threefold cornerstone of human dignity, solidarity and subsidiarity".[202] The globalized economy must be analyzed in the light of the principles of social justice, respecting the preferential option for the poor who must be allowed to take their place in such an economy, and the requirements of the international common good. For "the Church's social doctrine is a moral vision which aims to encourage governments, institutions and private organizations to shape a future consonant with the dignity of every person. Within this perspective it is possible to examine questions of external debt, internal political corruption and discrimination both within and between nations".[203]

---

[201] *Propositio* 69.
[202] *Propositio* 74.
[203] *Ibid.*

The Church in America is called not only to promote greater integration between nations, thus helping to create an authentic globalized culture of solidarity,[204] but also to cooperate with every legitimate means in reducing the negative effects of globalization, such as the domination of the powerful over the weak, especially in the economic sphere, and the loss of the values of local cultures in favor of a misconstrued homogenization.

Social sins which cry to heaven

56.   The Church's social doctrine also makes possible a clearer appreciation of the gravity of the "social sins which cry to heaven because they generate violence, disrupt peace and harmony between communities within single nations, between nations and between the different regions of the continent".[205] Among these must be mentioned: "the drug trade, the recycling of illicit funds, corruption at every level, the terror of violence, the arms race, racial discrimination, inequality between social groups and the irrational destruction of nature".[206] These sins are the sign of a deep crisis caused by the loss of a sense of God and the absence of those moral principles which should guide the life of every person. In the absence of moral points of reference, an unbridled

---

[204] Cf. *Propositio* 67.
[205] *Propositio* 70.
[206] *Ibid*.

greed for wealth and power takes over, obscuring any Gospel-based vision of social reality.

Not infrequently, this leads some public institutions to ignore the actual social climate. More and more, in many countries of America, a system known as "neoliberalism" prevails; based on a purely economic conception of man, this system considers profit and the law of the market as its only parameters, to the detriment of the dignity of and the respect due to individuals and peoples. At times this system has become the ideological justification for certain attitudes and behavior in the social and political spheres leading to the neglect of the weaker members of society. Indeed, the poor are becoming ever more numerous, victims of specific policies and structures which are often unjust.[207]

On the basis of the Gospel, the best response to this tragic situation is the promotion of solidarity and peace, with a view to achieving real justice. For this to happen, encouragement and support must be given to all those who are examples of honesty in the administration of public finances and of justice. So too there is a need to support the process of democratization presently taking place in America,[208] since a democratic system provides greater control over potential abuses.

"The rule of law is the necessary condition for the establishment of an authentic democra-

---

[207] Cf. *Propositio* 73.
[208] Cf. *Propositio* 70.

cy".[209] For democracy to develop, there is a need for civic education and the promotion of public order and peace. In effect, "there is no authentic and stable democracy without social justice. Thus the Church needs to pay greater attention to the formation of consciences, which will prepare the leaders of society for public life at all levels, promote civic education, respect for law and for human rights, and inspire greater efforts in the ethical training of political leaders".[210]

The ultimate foundation of human rights

57.   It is appropriate to recall that the foundation on which all human rights rest is the dignity of the person. "God's masterpiece, man, is made in the divine image and likeness. Jesus took on our human nature, except for sin; he advanced and defended the dignity of every human person, without exception; he died that all might be free. The Gospel shows us how Christ insisted on the centrality of the human person in the natural order (cf. *Lk* 12:22-29) and in the social and religious orders, even against the claims of the Law (cf. *Mk* 2:27): defending men, women (cf. *Jn* 8:11) and even children (cf. *Mt* 19:13-15), who in his time and culture occupied an inferior place in society. The human being's dignity as a child of God is the source of human rights and of cor-

[209] *Propositio* 72.
[210] *Ibid.*

responding duties".[211] For this reason, "every offense against the dignity of man is an offense against God himself, in whose image man is made".[212] This dignity is common to all, without exception, since all have been created in the image of God (cf. *Gen* 1:26). Jesus' answer to the question "Who is my neighbor?" (*Lk* 10:29) demands of each individual an attitude of respect for the dignity of others and of real concern for them, even if they are strangers or enemies (cf. *Lk* 10:30-37). In all parts of America the awareness that human rights must be respected has increased in recent times, yet much still remains to be done, if we consider the violations of the rights of persons and groups still taking place on the continent.

Preferential love for the poor and the outcast

58.   "The Church in America must incarnate in her pastoral initiatives the solidarity of the universal Church towards the poor and the outcast of every kind. Her attitude needs to be one of assistance, promotion, liberation and fraternal openness. The goal of the Church is to ensure that no one is marginalized".[213] The memory of the dark chapters of America's history, involving the practice of slavery and other situations of so-

[211] *Ibid.*

[212] THIRD GENERAL CONFERENCE OF THE LATIN AMERICAN BISHOPS, Puebla 1979, *Message to the Peoples of Latin America*, No. 306.

[213] *Propositio* 73.

cial discrimination, must awaken a sincere desire for conversion leading to reconciliation and communion.

Concern for those most in need springs from a decision to love the poor in a special manner. This is a love which is not exclusive and thus cannot be interpreted as a sign of partiality or sectarianism; [214] in loving the poor the Christian imitates the attitude of the Lord, who during his earthly life devoted himself with special compassion to all those in spiritual and material need.

The Church's work on behalf of the poor in every part of America is important; yet efforts are still needed to make this line of pastoral activity increasingly directed to an encounter with Christ who, though rich, made himself poor for our sakes, that he might enrich us by his poverty (cf. *2 Cor* 8:9). There is a need to intensify and broaden what is already being done in this area, with the goal of reaching as many of the poor as possible. Sacred Scripture reminds us that God hears the cry of the poor (cf. *Ps* 34:7) and the Church must heed the cry of those most in need. Hearing their voice, "she must live with the poor and share their distress. By her lifestyle her priorities, her words and her actions, she must testify that she is in communion and solidarity with them".[215]

---

[214] Cf. CONGREGATION FOR THE DOCTRINE OF THE FAITH, Instruction *Libertatis Conscientia* (March 22, 1986), 68: *AAS* 79 (1987), 583-584.

[215] *Propositio* 73.

59. The existence of a foreign debt which is suffocating quite a few countries of the American continent represents a complex problem. While not entering into its many aspects, the Church in her pastoral concern cannot ignore this difficult situation, since it touches the life of so many people. For this reason, different Episcopal Conferences in America, conscious of the gravity of the question, have organized study meetings on the subject and have published documents aimed at pointing out workable solutions.[216] I too have frequently expressed my concern about this situation, which in some cases has become unbearable. In light of the imminent Great Jubilee of the Year 2000, and recalling the social significance that Jubilees had in the Old Testament, I wrote: "In the spirit of the Book of Leviticus (25:8-12), Christians will have to raise their voice on behalf of all the poor of the world, proposing the Jubilee as an appropriate time to give thought, among other things, to reducing substantially, if not cancelling outright, the international debt which seriously threatens the future of many nations".[217]

Once more I express the hope, which the Synod Fathers made their own, that the Pontifical Council for Justice and Peace together with

[216] Cf. *Propositio* 75.
[217] Apostolic Letter *Tertio Millennio Adveniente* (November 10, 1994), 51: *AAS* 87 (1995), 36.

other competent agencies, such as the Section for Relations with States of the Secretariat of State, "through study and dialogue with representatives of the First World and with the leaders of the World Bank and the International Monetary Fund, will seek ways of resolving the problem of the foreign debt and produce guidelines that would prevent similar situations from recurring on the occasion of future loans".[218] On the broadest level possible, it would be helpful if "internationally known experts in economics and monetary questions would undertake a critical analysis of the world economic order, in its positive and negative aspects, so as to correct the present order, and that they would propose a system and mechanisms capable of ensuring an integral and concerted development of individuals and peoples".[219]

The fight against corruption

60.   In America too, the phenomenon of corruption is widespread. The Church can effectively help to eradicate this evil from civil society by "the greater involvement of competent Christian laity who, thanks to their training in the family, at school and in the parish, foster the practice of values such as truth, honesty, industriousness and the service of the common good".[220] In order to

[218] *Propositio* 75.
[219] *Ibid.*
[220] *Propositio* 37.

100

attain this goal, and to offer enlightenment to all people of good will anxious to put an end to the evils resulting from corruption, there is a need to teach and make known as widely as possible the passages of the *Catechism of the Catholic Church* devoted to this subject, while making Catholics in the different nations better acquainted with the relevant documents published by Episcopal Conferences in other countries.[221] With such training, Christians will contribute significantly to resolving the problem of corruption, committing themselves to put into practice the Church's social doctrine in all matters affecting their lives and in those areas where they can be of help to others.

The drug problem

61.　With regard to the serious problem of the drug trade, the Church in America can cooperate effectively with national and business leaders, non-governmental organizations and international agencies in developing projects aimed at doing away with this trade which threatens the well-being of the peoples of America.[222] This cooperation must be extended to legislative bodies, in support of initiatives to prevent the "recycling of funds", foster control of the assets of those involved in this traffic, and ensure that the production and

[221] Cf. *ibid.* Regarding the publication of these texts, cf. JOHN PAUL II, Apostolic Letter Issued "Motu Proprio" *Apostolos Suos* (May 21, 1998), IV: *AAS* 90 (1998), 657-658.
[222] Cf. *Propositio* 38.

marketing of the chemical substances from which drugs are obtained are carried out according to the law. The urgency and the gravity of the problem make it imperative to call upon the various sectors and groups within civil society to be united in the fight against the drug trade.[223] Specifically, as far as the Bishops are concerned, it is necessary — as the Synod Fathers suggested — that they themselves, as Pastors of the People of God, courageously and forcefully condemn the hedonism, materialism and life styles which easily lead to drug use.[224]

There is also a need to help poor farmers from being tempted by the easy money gained from cultivating plants used for drug-production. In this regard international agencies can make a valuable contribution to governments by providing incentives to encourage the production of alternative crops. Encouragement must also be given to those involved in rehabilitating drug users and to those engaged in the pastoral care of the victims of drug dependence. It is fundamentally important to offer the proper "meaning of life" to young people who, when faced with a lack of such meaning, not infrequently find themselves caught in the destructive spiral of drugs. Experience shows that this work of recuperation and

[223] Cf. *ibid.*
[224] *Ibid.*

social rehabilitation can be an authentic commitment to evangelization.[225]

The arms race

62. One factor seriously paralyzing the progress of many nations in America is the arms race. The particular Churches in America must raise a prophetic voice to condemn the arms race and the scandalous arms trade, which consumes huge sums of money which should instead be used to combat poverty and promote development.[226] On the other hand, the stockpiling of weapons is a cause of instability and a threat to peace.[227] For this reason the Church remains vigilant in situations where these is a risk of armed conflict, even between sister nations. As a sign and instrument of reconciliation and peace, she must seek "by every means possible, including mediation and arbitration, to act in favor of peace and fraternity between peoples".[228]

The culture of death and a society dominated by the powerful

63. Nowadays, in America as elsewhere in the world, a model of society appears to be emerging

---

[225] Cf. *ibid.*

[226] Cf. PONTIFICAL COUNCIL FOR JUSTICE AND PEACE, *The International Arms Trade. An Ethical Reflection* (May 1, 1994): *Enchiridion Vaticanum* 14, 1071-1154.

[227] Cf. *Propositio* 76.

[228] *Ibid.*

in which the powerful predominate, setting aside and even eliminating the powerless: I am thinking here of unborn children, helpless victims of abortion; the elderly and incurably ill, subjected at times to euthanasia; and the many other people relegated to the margins of society by consumerism and materialism. Nor can I fail to mention the unnecessary recourse to the death penalty when other "bloodless means are sufficient to defend human lives against an aggressor and to protect public order and the safety of persons. Today, given the means at the State's disposal to deal with crime and control those who commit it, without abandoning all hope of their redemption, the cases where it is absolutely necessary to do away with an offender 'are now very rare, even non-existent practically'".[229] This model of society bears the stamp of the culture of death, and is therefore in opposition to the Gospel message. Faced with this distressing reality, the Church community intends to commit itself all the more to the defense of the culture of life.

In this regard, the Synod Fathers, echoing recent documents of the Church's Magisterium, forcefully restated their unconditional respect for and total dedication to human life from the moment of conception to that of natural death, and their condemnation of evils like abortion and euthanasia. If the teachings of the divine and natu-

---

[229] *Catechism of the Catholic Church*, No. 2267, which cites JOHN PAUL II, Encyclical Letter *Evangelium Vitae* (March 25, 1995), 56: *AAS* 87 (1995), 463-464.

ral law are to be upheld, it is essential to promote knowledge of the Church's social doctrine and to work so that the values of life and family are recognized and defended in social customs and in State ordinances.[230] As well as protecting life, greater efforts should be made, through a variety of pastoral initiatives, to promote adoptions and to provide continuing assistance to women with problem pregnancies, both before and after the birth of the child. Special pastoral attention must also be given to women who have undergone or actively procured an abortion.[231]

How can we fail to thank God and express genuine appreciation to our brothers and sisters in the faith throughout America who are committed, along with other Christians and countless individuals of good will, to defending life by every legal means and to protecting the unborn, the incurably ill and the handicapped? Their work is all the more praiseworthy if we consider the indifference of so many people, the threats posed by eugenics and the assaults on life and human dignity perpetrated everywhere each day.[232]

This same concern must be shown to the elderly, who are often neglected and left to fend for themselves. They must be respected as persons; it is important to care for them and to help them in ways which will promote their rights and ensure their greatest possible physical and spiritu-

[230] Cf. *Propositio* 13.
[231] Cf. *ibid.*
[232] Cf. *ibid.*

al well-being. The elderly must be protected from situations or pressures which could drive them to suicide; in particular they must be helped nowadays to resist the temptation of assisted suicide and euthanasia.

Together with the Pastors of the People of God in America, I appeal to "Catholics working in the field of medicine and health care, to those holding public office or engaged in teaching, to make every effort to defend those lives most at risk, and to act with a conscience correctly formed in accordance with Catholic doctrine. Here Bishops and priests have a special responsibility to bear tireless witness to the Gospel of life and to exhort the faithful to act accordingly".[233] At the same time, it is essential for the Church in America to take appropriate measures to influence the deliberations of legislative assemblies, encouraging citizens, both Catholics and other people of good will, to establish organizations to propose workable legislation and to resist measures which endanger the two inseparable realities of life and the family. Nowadays there is a special need to pay attention to questions related to prenatal diagnosis, in order to avoid any violation of human dignity.

Discrimination against indigenous peoples and Americans of African descent

64.   If the Church in America, in fidelity to the Gospel of Christ, intends to walk the path of

[233] *Ibid.*

solidarity, she must devote special attention to those ethnic groups which even today experience discrimination. Every attempt to marginalize the indigenous peoples must be eliminated. This means, first of all, respecting their territories and the pacts made with them; likewise, efforts must be made to satisfy their legitimate social, health and cultural requirements. And how can we overlook the need for reconciliation between the indigenous peoples and the societies in which they are living?

Here I would like to mention that in some places Americans of African descent still suffer from ethnic prejudice, and this represents a serious obstacle to their encounter with Christ. Since all people, whatever their race or condition, have been created by God in his image, it is necessary to encourage concrete programs, in which common prayer must play a part, aimed at promoting understanding and reconciliation between different peoples. These can build bridges of Christian love, peace and justice between all men and women.[234]

In order to attain these goals it is essential to train competent pastoral workers capable of employing methods already legitimately "inculturated" in catechesis and the liturgy, avoiding a syncretism which gives only a partial account of true Christian doctrine. Then too, it will be easier to provide a sufficient number of pastors to work

[234] Cf. *Propositio* 19.

with the native peoples if efforts are made to promote priestly and religious vocations within the midst of these very people.[235]

The question of immigrants

65.   In its history, America has experienced many immigrations, as waves of men and women came to its various regions in the hope of a better future. The phenomenon continues even today, especially with many people and families from Latin American countries who have moved to the northern parts of the continent, to the point where in some cases they constitute a substantial part of the population. They often bring with them a cultural and religious heritage which is rich in Christian elements. The Church is well aware of the problems created by this situation and is committed to spare no effort in developing her own pastoral strategy among these immigrant people, in order to help them settle in their new land and to foster a welcoming attitude among the local population, in the belief that a mutual openness will bring enrichment to all.

Church communities will not fail to see in this phenomenon a specific call to live an evangelical fraternity and at the same time a summons to strengthen their own religious spirit with a view to a more penetrating evangelization. With this in mind, the Synod Fathers recalled

[235] Cf. *Propositio* 18.

that "the Church in America must be a vigilant advocate, defending against any unjust restriction the natural right of individual persons to move freely within their own nation and from one nation to another. Attention must be called to the rights of migrants and their families and to respect for their human dignity, even in cases of non-legal immigration".[236]

Migrants should be met with a hospitable and welcoming attitude which can encourage them to become part of the Church's life, always with due regard for their freedom and their specific cultural identity. Cooperation between the dioceses from which they come and those in which they settle, also through specific pastoral structures provided for in the legislation and praxis of the Church,[237] has proved extremely beneficial to this end. In this way the most adequate and complete pastoral care possible can be ensured. The Church in America must be constantly concerned to provide for the effective evangelization of those recent arrivals who do not yet know Christ.[238]

[236] *Propositio* 20.

[237] Cf. CONGREGATION FOR BISHOPS, Instruction *Nemo Est* (August 22, 1969), No. 16: *AAS* 61 (1969), 621-622; *Code of Canon Law,* Canons 294 and 518; *Code of Canons of the Eastern Churches,* Canon 280 § 1.

[238] Cf. *ibid.*

CHAPTER VI

THE MISSION OF THE CHURCH IN AMERICA TODAY: THE NEW EVANGELIZATION

"As the Father has sent me, even so I send you" (*Jn* 20:21)

Sent by Christ

66.   The Risen Christ, before his Ascension into heaven, sent the Apostles to preach the Gospel to the whole world (cf. *Mk* 16:15) and conferred on them the powers needed to carry out this mission. It is significant that, before giving his final missionary mandate, Jesus should speak of the universal power he had received from the Father (cf. *Mt* 28:18). In effect, Christ passed on to the Apostles the mission which he had received from the Father (cf. *Jn* 20:21), and in this way gave them a share in his powers.

Yet "the lay faithful too, precisely as members of the Church, have the vocation and mission of proclaiming the Gospel: they are prepared for this work by the sacraments of Christian initiation and by the gifts of the Holy Spirit".[239] They have been "in their own way made sharers in the priestly, prophetic and kingly functions of Christ".[240] Consequently, "the lay faithful, in virtue of their participation in the prophetic mission of Christ, are fully part of this work of the Church"[241] and so should feel called and encouraged to proclaim the Good News of the Kingdom. Jesus' words: "You too, go into the vineyard" (*Mt* 20:4),[242] must be seen as addressed not only to the Apostles but to all who desire to be authentic disciples of the Lord.

The basic task for which Jesus sends out his disciples is the proclamation of the Good News, that is, evangelization (cf. *Mk* 16:15-18). Consequently, "to evangelize is the grace and vocation proper to the Church, her most profound identity".[243] As I have said on other occasions, the new and unique situation in which the world and the Church find themselves at the threshold of the Third Millennium, and the urgent needs which result, mean that the mission of evangelization today calls for a new program which can be defined overall as a "new evangelization".[244] As the

[239] JOHN PAUL II, Post-Synodal Apostolic Exhortation *Christifideles Laici* (December 30, 1988), 33: *AAS* 81 (1989), 453.

[240] SECOND VATICAN ECUMENICAL COUNCIL, Dogmatic Constitution on the Church *Lumen Gentium*, 31.

[241] JOHN PAUL II, Post-Synodal Apostolic Exhortation *Christifideles Laici* (December 30, 1988), 34: *AAS* 81 (1989), 455.

[242] Cf. *ibid.*, 2, *loc. cit.*, 394-397.

[243] PAUL VI, Apostolic Exhortation *Evangelii Nuntiandi* (December 8, 1975), 14: *AAS* 68 (1976), 13.

[244] Cf. Post-Synodal Apostolic Exhortation *Christifideles Laici* (December 30, 1988), 34: *AAS* 81 (1989), 455.

Church's Supreme Pastor, I urgently desire to encourage all the members of God's People, particularly those living in America — where I first appealed for a commitment "new in its ardor, methods and expression" [245] — to take up this project and to cooperate in carrying it out. In accepting this mission, everyone should keep in mind that the vital core of the new evangelization must be a clear and unequivocal proclamation of the person of Jesus Christ, that is, the preaching of his name, his teaching, his life, his promises and the Kingdom which he has gained for us by his Paschal Mystery.[246]

Jesus Christ, the "good news"
and the prime evangelizer

67.   Jesus Christ is the "good news" of salvation made known to people yesterday, today and for ever; but he is also the first and greatest evangelizer.[247] The Church must make the crucified and risen Christ the center of her pastoral concern and her evangelizing activity. "Everything planned in the Church must have Christ and his Gospel as its starting-point".[248] Therefore, "the Church in America must speak increasingly of

[245] Address to the Assembly of CELAM (March 9, 1983), III: *AAS* 75 (1983), 778.

[246] Cf. PAUL VI, Apostolic Exhortation *Evangelii Nuntiandi*, 22: *AAS* 68 (1976), 20.

[247] Cf. *ibid.*, 7: *loc. cit.*, 9-10.

[248] JOHN PAUL II, Message to CELAM (September 14, 1997), 6: *L'Osservatore Romano*, October 1, 1997, p. 4.

Jesus Christ, the human face of God and the divine face of man. It is this proclamation that truly makes an impact on people, awakens and transforms hearts, in a word, converts. Christ must be proclaimed with joy and conviction, but above all by the witness of each one's life".[249]

Individual Christians will be able to carry out their mission effectively to the extent that they make the life of the Son of God made man the perfect model for their work of spreading the Gospel. The simplicity of his manner and his choices must be normative for everyone in the work of evangelization. In this perspective, the poor will certainly be considered among the first to be evangelized, following the example of Christ, who said of himself: "The Spirit of the Lord . . . has anointed me to preach good news to the poor" (*Lk* 4:18).[250]

As I have already noted, love for the poor must be preferential, but not exclusive. The Synod Fathers observed that it was in part because of an approach to the pastoral care of the poor marked by a certain exclusiveness that the pastoral care for the leading sectors of society has been neglected and many people have thus been estranged from the Church.[251] The damage done by the spread of secularism in these sectors — political or economic, union-related, military, social or cultural — shows how urgent it is that

[249] *Propositio* 8.
[250] Cf. *Propositio* 57.
[251] Cf. *Propositio* 16.

they be evangelized, with the encouragement and guidance of the Church's Pastors, who are called by God to care for everyone. They will be able to count on the help of those who — fortunately still numerous — have remained faithful to Christian values. In this regard the Synod Fathers have recognized "the commitment of many leaders to building a just and fraternal society".[252] With their support, Pastors will face the not easy task of evangelizing these sectors of society. With renewed fervor and updated methods, they will announce Christ to leaders, men and women alike, insisting especially on the formation of consciences on the basis of the Church's social doctrine. This formation will act as the best antidote to the not infrequent cases of inconsistency and even corruption marking socio-political structures. Conversely, if this evangelization of the leadership sector is neglected, it should not come as a surprise that many who are a part of it will be guided by criteria alien to the Gospel and at times openly contrary to it.

The encounter with Christ spurs evangelization

68.　An encounter with the Lord brings about a profound transformation in all who do not close themselves off from him. The first impulse coming from this transformation is to communicate to others the richness discovered in the ex-

[252] *Ibid.*

perience of the encounter. This does not mean simply teaching what we have come to know but also, like the Samaritan woman, enabling others to encounter Jesus personally: "Come and see" (*Jn* 4:29). The result will be the same as that which took place in the heart of the Samaritans, who said to the woman: "It is no longer because of your words that we believe, for we have heard for ourselves, and we know that this is indeed the Savior of the world" (*Jn* 4:42). The Church, which draws her life from the permanent and mysterious presence of her Risen Lord, has as the core of her mission a duty "to lead all people to encounter Christ".[253]

She is called to proclaim that Christ is indeed the Living One, the Son of God, who became man, died and rose again. He alone is the Savior of every person and of the whole person; as the Lord of history, he is constantly at work in the Church and in the world through his Spirit, until the end of time. This presence of the Risen One in the Church makes it possible for us to encounter him, thanks to the invisible working of his life-giving Spirit. This encounter takes place in the faith received from and lived in the Church, the Mystical Body of Christ. The encounter with Christ then has an essentially ecclesial dimension, and it leads to a life commitment. Indeed, "to encounter the living Christ means to accept the love by which he loves us first, to

[253] *Propositio* 2.

choose him, to adhere freely to his person and his plan, which consists in proclaiming and in bringing about the Kingdom of God".[254]

The calling gives rise to a search for Jesus: "'Rabbi' (which means Teacher), 'where are you staying'. He said to them: 'Come and see'. They came and saw where he was staying; and they stayed that day with him" (*Jn* 1:38-39). This "staying" is not limited to the day of one's call, but rather extends to the whole of life. To follow Jesus involves living as he lived, accepting his message, adopting his way of thinking, embracing his destiny and sharing his project, which is the plan of the Father: it involves inviting everyone to communion with the Trinity and to communion among ourselves in a just and fraternal society".[255] The burning desire to invite others to encounter the One whom we have encountered is the start of the evangelizing mission to which the whole Church is called. This mission has become particularly urgent today in America, five hundred years after the first evangelization, as we prepare to commemorate with gratitude the two thousandth anniversary of the coming of the only-begotten Son of God into the world.

The importance of catechesis

69.   The new evangelization in which the whole continent is engaged means that faith can-

[254]   *Ibid.*
[255]   *Ibid.*

not be taken for granted, but must be explicitly proposed in all its breadth and richness. This is the principal objective of catechesis, which, by its very nature, is an essential aspect of the new evangelization. "Catechesis is a process of formation in faith, hope and charity; it shapes the mind and touches the heart, leading the person to embrace Christ fully and completely. It introduces the believer more fully into the experience of the Christian life, which involves the liturgical celebration of the mystery of the Redemption and the Christian service of others".[256]

Well realizing the need for a complete catechesis, I made my own the proposal of the Fathers of the 1985 Extraordinary Assembly of the Synod of Bishops to compose "a catechism or compendium of all Catholic doctrine regarding both faith and morals", which could serve as "a point of reference for the catechisms or compendia that are prepared in the various regions".[257] This proposal was implemented with the publication of the typical edition of the *Catechismus Catholicae Ecclesiae*.[258] In addition to the text of the Catechism, and for a better utilization of its contents, I intended that a *General Directory for Catechesis* should also be compiled and published.[259] I hearti-

[256] *Propositio* 10.

[257] Final Report *Ecclesia sub Verbo Dei Mysteria Christi Celebrans pro Salute Mundi (December 7, 1985), II, B, a, 4: Enchiridion Vaticanum* 9, 1797.

[258] Cf. Apostolic Letter *Laetamur Magnopere* (August 15, 1997): *AAS* 89 (1997), 819-821.

[259] CONGREGATION FOR THE CLERGY, *General Directory for Catechesis*, Libreria Editrice Vaticana, 1997.

ly recommend the use of these two resources, of universal value, to everyone involved in catechesis in America. It is to be hoped that both documents will be employed "in the preparation and the evaluation of all parochial and diocesan programs of catechesis, bearing in mind that the religious situation of young people and adults calls for a catechesis which is more kerygmatic and more organic in its presentation of the contents of the faith".[260]

It is necessary to acknowledge and encourage the outstanding work done by so many catechists throughout America as authentic messengers of the kingdom: "Their faith and their witness of life are an integral part of catechesis".[261] I wish all the more to encourage the faithful to take up, with commitment and love of the Lord, this service to the Church, generously offering their time and their talents. Bishops for their part should be concerned that catechists receive appropriate formation to enable them to carry out this task, so indispensable in the life of the Church.

In catechesis it will be useful to keep in mind, especially on a continent like America where the social question takes on such importance, that "growth in the understanding of the faith and its practical expression in social life are intimately connected. Efforts made to favor an encounter with Christ cannot fail to have a posi-

---

[260] *Propositio* 10.
[261] *Ibid.*

tive repercussion in the promotion of the common good in a just society".[262]

The evangelization of culture

70.   My Predecessor Paul VI widely remarked that "the split between the Gospel and culture is undoubtedly the drama of our time".[263] Hence the Synod Fathers rightly felt that "the new evangelization calls for a clearly conceived, serious and well organized effort to evangelize culture".[264] The Son of God, by taking upon himself our human nature, became incarnate within a particular people, even though his redemptive death brought salvation to all people, of every culture, race and condition. The gift of his Spirit and his love are meant for each and every people and culture, in order to bring them all into unity after the example of the perfect unity existing in the Triune God. For this to happen, it is necessary to inculturate preaching in such a way that the Gospel is proclaimed in the language and in the culture of its hearers.[265] At the same time, however, it must not be forgotten that the Paschal Mystery of Christ, the supreme manifestation of the infinite God within the finitude of history, is the only valid point of reference for all of humanity on its

[262] *Ibid.*
[263] Apostolic Exhortation *Evangelii Nuntiandi* (December 8, 1975), 20: *AAS* 68 (1976), 19.
[264] *Propositio* 17.
[265] Cf. *ibid.*

119

pilgrimage in search of authentic unity and true peace.

In America, the *mestiza* face of the Virgin of Guadalupe was from the start a symbol of the inculturation of the Gospel, of which she has been the lodestar and the guide. Through her powerful intercession, the Gospel will penetrate the hearts of the men and women of America and permeate their cultures, transforming them from within.[266]

Evangelizing centers of education

71.   Education can play an outstanding role in promoting the inculturation of the Gospel. Nonetheless, Catholic centers of education, and those which, although non-denominational, are clearly inspired by Catholic principles, will be able to engage in authentic evangelization only if at all levels — including that of the university — they clearly preserve their Catholic orientation. The content of the education they impart should make constant reference to Jesus Christ and his message as the Church presents it in her dogmatic and moral teaching. Only in this way will they train truly Christian leaders in the different spheres of human activity, and in society, especially in politics, economics, science, art and philosophical reflection.[267] Hence, "it is essential that the Catholic university be truly both things

[266] Cf. *ibid*.
[267] Cf. *Propositio* 22.

at once: a university and Catholic. Its Catholic character is an essential element of the university as an institution, and therefore does not depend simply on the decision of the individuals who govern the university at any particular time".[268] Pastoral work in Catholic universities will therefore be given special attention: it must encourage a commitment to the apostolate on the part of the students themselves, so that they can become the evangelizers of the university world.[269] In addition, "cooperation between Catholic universities throughout America needs to be encouraged, for their mutual enrichment";[270] this will help put into effect, at the university level too, the principle of solidarity and interchange between the peoples of the whole continent.

Something similar must also be said about Catholic schools, particularly with regard to secondary education: "A special effort should be made to strengthen the Catholic identity of schools, whose specific character is based on an educational vision having its origin in the person of Christ and its roots in the teachings of the Gospel. Catholic schools must seek not only to impart a quality education from the technical and professional standpoint, but also and above all provide for the integral formation of the human person.[271] Given the importance of the work done

[268] *Propositio* 23.
[269] Cf. *ibid.*
[270] *Ibid.*
[271] *Propositio* 24.

by Catholic educators, I join the Synod Fathers in gratefully encouraging all those devoted to teaching in Catholic schools — priests, consecrated men and women and committed lay people — "to persevere in their most important mission".[272] The influence of these educational centers should extend to all sectors of society, without distinction or exclusion. It is essential that every possible effort be made to ensure that Catholic schools, despite financial difficulties, continue to provide "a Catholic education to the poor and the marginalized in society".[273] It will never be possible to free the needy from their poverty unless they are first freed from the impoverishment arising from the lack of adequate education.

In the overall work of the new evangelization, the educational sector occupies a place of honor. For this reason, the activity of all Catholic teachers, including those working in non-denominational schools, should be encouraged. I also make an urgent appeal to men and women religious not to abandon this field which is so important for the new evangelization.[274]

As a fruit and an expression of the communion existing between all the particular Churches of America, certainly strengthened by the spiritual experience of the Synodal Assembly, an effort must be made to promote gatherings of Catholic

272 *Ibid.*
273 *Ibid.*
274 Cf. *Propositio* 22.

educators at the national and continental levels, in an attempt to coordinate and expand the educational apostolate in every context.[275]

To carry out these tasks, the Church in America requires a degree of freedom in the field of education; this is not to be seen as a privilege but as a right, in virtue of the evangelizing mission entrusted to the Church by the Lord. Furthermore, parents have a fundamental and primary right to make decisions about the education of their children; consequently, Catholic parents must be able to choose an education in harmony with their religious convictions. The function of the State in this area is subsidiary; the State has the duty "to ensure that education is available to all and to respect and defend freedom of instruction. A State monopoly in this area must be condemned as a form of totalitarianism which violates the fundamental rights which it ought to defend, especially the right of parents to provide religious education for their children. The family is the place where the education of the person primarily takes place".[276]

Evangelization through the media

72.   For the new evangelization to be effective, it is essential to have a deep understanding of the culture of our time in which the social communications media are most influential. There-

[275] Cf. *ibid.*
[276] *Ibid.*

fore, knowledge and use of the media, whether the more traditional forms or those which technology has produced in recent times, is indispensable. Contemporary reality demands a capacity to learn the language, nature and characteristics of mass media. Using the media correctly and competently can lead to a genuine inculturation of the Gospel. At the same time, the media also help to shape the culture and mentality of people today, which is why there must be special pastoral activity aimed at those working in the media.[277]

On this point, the Synod Fathers suggested a range of concrete initiatives to make the Gospel effectively present in the world of social communications: the training of pastoral workers for this task; the support of high-quality production centers; the careful and effective use of satellite and other new technologies; teaching the faithful to be "critical" in their use of the media; joining forces in order to acquire and manage new transmitters and TV and radio networks, as well as coordinating those already in operation. Catholic publications also deserve support and need to develop the excellence sought by all.

Business people should be encouraged to provide economic support for quality products promoting human and Christian values.[278] But a program as vast as this is far beyond the resources of the individual particular Churches of the

[277] Cf. *Propositio* 25.
[278] Cf. *Ibid.*

American continent. Therefore, the Synod Fathers proposed an inter-American coordination of current activities in the field of social communications, aimed at fostering mutual awareness and coordination of current projects in the field.[279]

The challenge of the sects

73. The proselytizing activity of the sects and new religious groups in many parts of America is a grave hindrance to the work of evangelization. The word "proselytism" has a negative meaning when it indicates a way of winning followers which does not respect the freedom of those to whom a specific kind of religious propaganda is directed.[280] The Catholic Church in America is critical of proselytism by the sects and, for this reason, rejects methods of this kind in her own evangelizing work. Presenting the Gospel of Christ in its entirety, the work of evangelization must respect the inner sanctuary of every individual's conscience, where the decisive and absolutely personal dialogue between grace and human freedom unfolds.

This must be borne in mind especially with regard to the sisters and brothers of the Churches and Ecclesial Communities separated from the Catholic Church, long-established in some regions. The bonds of true though imperfect communion which, according to the teaching of the

[279] Cf. *Ibid.*
[280] Cf. *Instrumentum Laboris*, 45.

Second Vatican Council,[281] these communities already have with the Catholic Church must enlighten the attitudes of the Church and her members towards them.[282] These attitudes, however, must not be such that they weaken the firm conviction that only in the Catholic Church is found the fullness of the means of salvation established by Jesus Christ.[283]

The success of proselytism by sects and new religious groups in America cannot be ignored. It demands of the Church on the continent a thorough study, to be carried out in each nation and at the international level, to ascertain why many Catholics leave the Church. Pastoral policies will have to be revised, so that each particular Church can offer the faithful more personalized religious care, strengthen the structures of communion and mission, make the most of the evangelizing possibilities of a purified popular religiosity, and thus give new life to every Catholic's faith in Jesus Christ, through prayer and meditation upon the word of God, suitably explained.[284] No one can deny the urgency of prompt evangelizing efforts aimed at those segments of the People of God most exposed to proselytism by the sects: immigrants, neighborhoods on the outskirts of the cities or rural towns with no regular pres-

---

[281] Cf. Decree on Ecumenism *Unitatis Redintegratio*, 3.

[282] Cf. *Propositio* 64.

[283] Cf. SECOND VATICAN ECUMENICAL COUNCIL, Decree on Ecumenism *Unitatis Redintegratio*, 3.

[284] Cf. *Propositio* 65.

ence of a priest and therefore marked by widespread religious ignorance, families of simple people suffering from material difficulties of various kinds. From this point of view too, base-communities, movements, family groups and other forms of association in which it is easier to build interpersonal bonds of mutual support, both spiritual and economic, have shown themselves to be very helpful.

Moreover, as some of the Synod Fathers indicated, it is necessary to ask whether a pastoral strategy directed almost exclusively to meeting people's material needs has not in the end left their hunger for God unsatisfied, making them vulnerable to anything which claims to be of spiritual benefit. Hence, "it is indispensable that all remain united to Christ by means of a joyful and transforming kerygma, especially in liturgical preaching".[285] A Church which fervently lives the spiritual and contemplative dimension, and which gives herself generously to the service of charity, will be an ever more eloquent witness to God for men and women searching for meaning in their lives.[286] To this end, it is more necessary than ever for all the faithful to move from a faith of habit, sustained perhaps by social context alone, to a faith which is conscious and personally lived. The renewal of faith will always be the best way to lead others to the Truth that is Christ.

[285] *Ibid.*
[286] Cf. FOURTH GENERAL CONFERENCE OF THE LATIN AMERICAN BISHOPS, Santo Domingo, October 1992: *New Evangelization, Human Promotion and Christian Culture*, 139-152.

For the response to the challenge of the sects to be effective, there is a need for an appropriate coordination of initiatives among dioceses, aimed at bringing about a more effective cooperation through shared projects which will produce better results.[287]

The *mission* ad gentes

74.   Jesus Christ entrusted to his Church the mission of evangelizing all nations: "Go therefore and teach all nations, baptizing them in the name of the Father and of the Son and of the Holy Spirit, teaching them to observe all that I have commanded you" (*Mt* 28:19-20). There must always be a dynamic awareness of the universality of the evangelizing mission which the Church has received, as there has been consistently throughout the history of the pilgrim People of God in America. Evangelization is most urgent among those on this continent who do not yet know the name of Jesus, the only name given to men and women that they may be saved (cf. *Acts* 4:12). Unfortunately, the name of Jesus is unknown to a vast part of humanity and in many sectors of American society. It is enough to think of the indigenous peoples not yet Christianized or of the presence of non-Christian religions such as Islam, Buddhism or Hinduism, especially among immigrants from Asia.

[287] Cf. *Propositio* 65.

This obliges the Church in America to be involved in the mission *ad gentes*.[288] The program of a new evangelization on the American continent, to which many pastoral projects are directed, cannot be restricted to revitalizing the faith of regular believers, but must strive as well to proclaim Christ where he is not known.

Likewise, the particular Churches in America are called to extend their missionary efforts beyond the bounds of the continent. They cannot keep for themselves the immense riches of their Christian heritage. They must take this heritage to the whole world and share it with those who do not yet know it. Here it is a question of many millions of men and women who, without faith, suffer the most serious kind of poverty. Faced with this poverty, it would be a mistake not to encourage an evangelizing effort beyond the continent with the excuse that there is still much to do in America or to wait until the Church in America reaches the point, basically utopian, of full maturity.

With the hope that the American continent, in accordance with its Christian vitality, will play its part in the great task of the mission *ad gentes*, I make my own the practical proposals presented by the Synod Fathers: "to maintain a greater cooperation between sister Churches; to send missionaries (priests, religious and lay faithful) within the continent and abroad; to strengthen or create

[288] Cf. *Propositio* 86.

missionary institutes; to encourage the missionary dimension of consecrated and contemplative life; to give greater impetus to mission promotion, training and organization".[289] I am sure that the pastoral zeal of the Bishops and of the sons and daughters of the Church throughout America will devise concrete plans, also at the international level, to implement with great dynamism and creativity these missionary proposals.

[289] *Ibid*.

CONCLUSION

With hope and gratitude

75. "I am with you always, to the end of the age" (*Mt* 28:20). Trusting in this promise of the Lord, the pilgrim Church in America prepares enthusiastically to meet the challenges of today's world and those that will come in the future. In the Gospel, the Good News of the Resurrection of the Lord is accompanied by the invitation to fear not (cf. *Mt* 28:5, 10). The Church in America wishes to walk in hope, as the Synod Fathers declared: "With serene trust in the Lord of history, the Church prepares to cross the threshold of the Third Millennium freed from prejudice, hesitation, selfishness, fear or doubt, and convinced of the fundamental and primary service which she must provide as a testimony to her fidelity to God and to the men and women of the continent".[290]

Furthermore, the Church in America feels especially impelled to walk in faith, responding with gratitude to the love of Jesus, "the merciful love of God made flesh (cf. *Jn* 3:16)".[291] The cele-

[290] *Propositio* 58.
[291] *Ibid.*

131

bration of the beginning of the Third Christian Millennium can be the right moment for the People of God in America to renew "their thanks for the great gift of faith",[292] which they first received five centuries ago. The year 1492, beyond its historical and political meaning, was the great year of grace when America welcomed the faith: a faith which proclaims the supreme gift of the Incarnation of the Son of God two thousand years ago, and which we will solemnly commemorate in the Great Jubilee now so close.

This twofold sense of hope and gratitude must accompany every pastoral action of the Church on the continent, permeating with the spirit of the Jubilee the various initiatives in the dioceses, parishes, religious communities, ecclesial movements, and the activities which will be organized at both regional and continental levels.[293]

Prayer to Jesus Christ for the families of America

76. I therefore invite all the Catholics of America to take an active part in the evangelizing initiatives which the Holy Spirit is stirring in every part of this immense continent, so full of resources and hopes for the future. In a special way, I invite Catholic families to be "domestic Churches",[294] in which the Christian faith is lived

[292] *Ibid.*
[293] Cf. *Ibid.*
[294] SECOND VATICAN ECUMENICAL COUNCIL, Dogmatic Constitution on the Church *Lumen Gentium*, 11.

and passed on to the young as a treasure, and where all pray together. If they live up to the ideal which God places before them, Catholic homes will be true centers of evangelization.

In concluding this Apostolic Exhortation, in which I have taken up the proposals of the Synod Fathers, I gladly welcome their suggestion to compose a prayer for the families of America.[295] I invite individuals, communities and ecclesial groups, wherever two or more gather in the Lord's name, to strengthen through prayer the spiritual bond between all American Catholics. Let everyone join in the prayer of the Successor of Peter, invoking Christ who is "the way of conversion, communion and solidarity in America":

We thank you, Lord Jesus,
because the Gospel of the Father's love,
with which you came to save the world,
has been proclaimed far and wide in America
as a gift of the Holy Spirit
that fills us with gladness.

We thank you for the gift of your Life,
which you have given us by loving us to the end:
your Life makes us children of God,
brothers and sisters to each other.
Increase, O Lord, our faith and our love for you,
present in all the tabernacles of the continent.

Grant us to be faithful witnesses
to your Resurrection

---

[295] *Propositio* 12.

for the younger generation of Americans,
so that, in knowing you, they may follow you
and find in you their peace and joy.
Only then will they know that they
are brothers and sisters
of all God's children scattered
throughout the world.

You who, in becoming man,
chose to belong to a human family,
teach families the virtues which filled with light
the family home of Nazareth.

May families always be united,
as you and the Father are one,
and may they be living witnesses
to love, justice and solidarity;
make them schools of respect,
forgiveness and mutual help,
so that the world may believe;
help them to be the source of vocations
to the priesthood and the consecrated life,
and all the other forms
of firm Christian commitment.

Protect your Church and the Successor of Peter,
to whom you, Good Shepherd, have entrusted
the task of feeding your flock.
Grant that the Church in America may flourish
and grow richer in the fruits of holiness.

Teach us to love your Mother, Mary,
as you loved her.
Give us strength to proclaim

your word with courage
in the work of the new evangelization,
so that the world may know new hope.
Our Lady of Guadalupe, Mother of America,
pray for us!

Given at Mexico City, January 22, in the year
1999, the twenty-first of my Pontificate.

Joannes Paulus II